"Sam Waldron has written a concise yet substantive explanation of what is necessary in order to be right with God. Repentance and faith are duties that the Bible sets before everyone who would be saved. Dr. Waldron shows what these duties are and how they are fulfilled. May God use this little book to open the eyes of many to see things as they really are and to turn from sin and trust Jesus Christ as Lord."

TOM ASCOL—PASTOR AND EXECUTIVE DIRECTOR OF FOUNDERS MINISTRIES

"In a day when so little is understood or taught about the nature of true repentance and saving faith, this brief work on the subject is indispensable. I recommend that every minister of the Gospel be diligent to study its contents and preach its truths to their congregations."

PAUL DAVID WASHER—DIRECTOR OF HEARTCRY MISSIONARY SOCIETY

"I highly commend this outstandingly clear exposition of the two basic requirements of eternal salvation, namely repentance and faith."

ERROLL HULSE—EDITOR OF REFORMATION TODAY

TWO THINGS

YOU MUST DO TO BE SAVED

SAMUEL WALDRON

CALVARY PRESS PUBLISHING
CALVARYPRESS.COM

Published by Calvary Press Publishing.
Visit us at: CalvaryPress.com

ISBN 978-1-879737-92-1

PRINTED IN THE USA

CONTENTS

PREFACE:

WHAT IS THIS BOOK FOR?

I am firmly convinced that books like this should be written to serve God and one's fellow human beings. I am, therefore, convinced that one should give potential readers a clear idea of what kind of book they are buying. There are few things quite as frustrating as spending valuable time reading a book only to discover that it is not the kind of book you thought it was, and it is not doing for you what you thought it would do.

So right here let me tell you what *The Two Things You Must Do To Be Saved* is for. Or rather let me begin by telling you what this book is *not* for. This book is not for simply giving away to most of your non-Christian friends without explanation. It is not in that sense an evangelistic tract or booklet. I hope it might help some of them if you gave it to them, but if you do that, you will probably need to sit down with them and help them understand what it teaches at some crucial points.

And that brings me to what this book *is* for. This book is intended to help you communicate the gospel clearly, accurately, and thus effectively to others. You can use it, I think, as a tool, help or basis for an evangelistic Bible study in which you teach the gospel to your friends using the gifts God has given you. You can also use this book—and this is the primary use I think it will have—to train Christians who want to learn how to more accurately and therefore powerfully communicate what the gospel requires to others. *In other words, while this book may be used as the basis for an evangelistic Bible study, it is mainly a Bible study for evangelists (and those who want to be!).*

This, then, is why I wrote this book. I want to have a part in the great missionary and evangelistic calling of the church of Jesus Christ. I want to help you fulfill a more effective role in that Great Commission. I believe that a church without a missionary and evangelistic heart is not a Christian church. I want your church to develop and be productive in its missionary and evangelistic calling.

Others are better than me at leading evangelistic Bible studies and telling friends about Christ than I am. I want to be better at that, but I see the gifts others have, admire them, and know I will never attain to their facility at sharing the gospel. I need—the church needs—people with such a facility and such a gift for sharing the gospel with unconverted friends. What I want do in this book is help the gifted Christians I have just mentioned—and all of us—to understand more accurately, speak more carefully, and thus share more powerfully the gospel of Jesus Christ.

Of course, there are some that depreciate the need for a careful and clear understanding of the gospel. *Let's just get out there, share what we know, and love people.* Well, we certainly need to be zealous, love people and show them that we love them. But our love is not the gospel. Nor is our zeal a substitute for the gospel which is the power of God unto salvation. If our zeal and love are not the gospel that is the power of God unto salvation (Romans 1:16-17), then the more clearly we know and communicate the gospel the better we can bring its power to bear upon the souls of men. A study like this is, thus, essential when vast areas of gospel truth are being eroded by the tide of biblical ignorance sweeping in all around us.

CHAPTER 1:

ON DOING

My purpose in writing this little book is help you to understand more clearly and so communicate more powerfully the gospel of Christ with particular emphasis on its requirements. The title of this book, *The Two Things You Must Do To Be Saved*, is my way of describing what a crucial text from the Word of God on this subject makes clear. Of course, I do not assume that all those who read these pages still need to be saved. But I do assume that no one will be saved unless they do the two things which the text I have in mind requires.

So what is the text of which I am speaking? It is Acts 20:21. In the NASB it is translated as follows:

> **Acts 20:21:** solemnly testifying to both Jews and Greeks of repentance toward God and faith in our Lord Jesus Christ

It is not difficult to see the two things in the text I am talking about. I intend to say (and show) that repentance toward God and faith in our Lord Jesus Christ are the two things everyone must do to be saved.

But before I can come to that task there are a couple of preliminary issues which I think I need to clear up to prevent confusion. (Confusion is the last thing we need when it comes to the two things you and I must do to be saved.) My goal is to be as clear as possible with a subject as important as this.

Here is the first issue I am concerned to clear up: *doing*. There are several misunderstandings of the word *do* in the title of this book. Let me make sure that you do not mistake what I am saying for any of them.

The Misunderstanding of Doing as "Works for Salvation"

Perhaps the best way to make the first misunderstanding of *doing* clear is by imagining a friendly objector. I imagine this objector saying to me something like this: "*Do*? What do you mean *do*? There is nothing we can or ought to *do* to be saved. Salvation is by God's grace, not by our doing."

I have a number of responses to this imaginary objector. The first is that in an important sense I wholly agree with him. The Bible does certainly teach that we are not saved by our own deeds or works. Typical of biblical teaching on this subject are the following texts:

> **Romans 4:4:** Now to the one who works, his wage is not credited as a favor, but as what is due. 5 But to the one who does not work, but believes in Him who justifies the ungodly, his faith is credited as righteousness...
>
> **Ephesians 2:8:** For by grace you have been saved through faith; and that not of yourselves, *it is* the gift of God; 9 not as a result of works, so that no one may boast.
>
> **Titus 3:5:** He saved us, not on the basis of deeds which we have done in righteousness, but according to His mercy, by the washing of regeneration and renewing by the Holy Spirit,

When Christ on the cross said, "It is finished!" (John 19:30), it really was finished. Salvation is by the perfect work of Christ. It is not by our very imperfect works. Salvation is, as the Reformation made clear, by grace alone, Christ alone, and faith alone. In an important sense the gospel is not in the first place about our doing anything to save ourselves. It is about what Christ did to save us!

How, then, do I dare to speak of "doing" anything to be saved? Good question! The simple answer is that both Acts 20:21 and many parallel texts require me so to speak. Here in Acts 20:21 the Word of God speaks of repentance and faith as the things the gospel requires of us if we are to be saved. These are not things God in Christ does for us. They are things we must do.

Now clearly we have a difficulty, don't we? Christ's work is finished. We are not saved by "deeds which we have done in righteousness." Yet there is something God calls on us to do. There are activities required—things to be done—in order to be saved by the gospel. To obscure this plain fact is to darken the way of salvation to the eyes of men.

Clearly, we must distinguish two kinds of doing. Perhaps I can illustrate it for you. One of my fellow pastors much prefers driving to flying. Suppose he had problems with his van driving from Kentucky to California—serious problems! Somewhere in Arizona the van must be towed to the nearest auto mechanic. In God's good providence, the man is a great mechanic, and after several hours the van is fixed.

Now listen to what the mechanic says when he hands my fellow pastor the key to his van: *"The job is done. There is nothing left to do. All you have to do is just start her up."* Do you see how silly it would be for my fellow pastor to say, "If there is nothing left to do, why do I need this key? Why do I have to start her up? Why do I have to do anything?" Everybody knows that the mechanic is talking about two completely different kinds of "doing." Fixing the van and turning the key are not same kind of doing at all.

Now this is perhaps a silly illustration, and it is certainly an inadequate one, but I hope it helps you get my point. There are activities required of us by the gospel. They are on a completely different level than the work of Christ. They merit nothing from God. They are themselves gifts of grace. They are the opposite of human achievements that contribute to Christ's finished work, but they are activities or conditions required of men in the gospel and in response to which God saves men.

Perhaps a biblical illustration will help you. Jesus tells the story in Luke 15 of a free-spirited and very selfish son who asks his wealthy father to give him the inheritance he has coming. Christians know this boy as "the prodigal son." The father complies with the wishes of this son. The son promptly packs his belongings and leaves for the attractions of what the Bible calls the "distant country," but what we might call the "big city." There the young man squanders everything on wild living and wild women. Eventually, of course, he experiences the results of such a way of life and ends up in desperate and humiliating poverty. There he is, a "good" Jewish boy, feeding someone's pigs.

What can he do about this miserable condition? In one sense, of course, he can do nothing. He has no resources. He has squandered his inheritance. He is in a hopeless condition. Nothing he can do can recompense the father for squandering his wealth and bringing terrible shame on the family.

On the other hand, there is something that the young man must do to be saved. He must return to the father's house. This will in no way repay the father for the wrongs the young man has done. If the father chooses to receive him back, it will be all of grace. Nevertheless, unless he actually gets up and returns to the father and the father's house, that grace will never be experienced or enjoyed.

There is, thus, set before us in the Bible two kinds of doing. One kind we must utterly reject, but another we must carefully embrace. It is crucially important to understand the difference between these two kinds of doing if we are to be saved and know we are saved. When I speak of the two things you must do to be saved, I am not speaking of "works for salvation." Neither am I speaking of a doing which merits, earns, or deserves salvation. It is not a doing which creates salvation, but a doing that receives it.

It may help you to know that the distinction between two kinds of doing of which I have been speaking is related to the well-known and important distinction between the law and the gospel. When I speak of doing to be saved, I do not mean doing what the law requires, but doing what the gospel requires. The law requires perfect and perpetual obedience for its approval and for it not to condemn you to God's eternal wrath. The gospel requires no such thing for salvation. For you to be accepted with God it simply requires repentance toward God and faith toward our Lord Jesus Christ.

Perhaps this will help you grasp the distinction I have in mind. Faithful Christian teachers have insisted that saving faith is (in one sense) passive. It does not earn or construct salvation. It simply receives and rests on a divinely constructed salvation. From this perspective faith is passive and not doing at all. Since, however, the human mind and will are active in receiving and resting on God's salvation, in another sense it is something the human must do.

The Misunderstanding of Doing as "Heartless Externalism"

There is another misunderstanding of "doing" which I am also anxious that each of my readers avoid. Please do not think that the "doing" of which I am speaking is the kind of doing which is separated from or done without the heart. Let me explain.

In recent years a popular athletic shoe company has used the slogan, "Just do it!" I am not certain exactly what this slogan is intended to convey. What it conveys to me, however, is this: Just do it—no matter how you feel about. Just do it—even if you do not feel like it. Just do it—even though your heart is not in it.

That may work in the realm of physical fitness, but it does not work in the realm of salvation. Let me make really clear that this is not the kind of doing of which I am speaking. As will become clear in the following pages, the doing of Acts 20:21 is exactly and precisely a heart-doing. It is, in other words, a doing that is done in the heart and with the heart. Both repentance and faith are heart activities. They are not a kind of mindless jumping through external hoops. They are not heartless routines. They are wholesouled and wholehearted activities. In the gospel call for faith and repentance God is saying like the father in the Book of Proverbs, *My son, give me your heart*. Heartless externalism will save no one. The *doing* of heartless externalism will save no one.

Hence, as I will also make clear in the pages ahead, these activities, though human activities, are not activities that arise from unrenewed hearts. We will see that the arrow of faith is drawn only from the quiver of God's sovereign grace. The tree of repentance, we will prove, grows only in the soil of a renewed heart. Thus, these activities of repentance and faith only arise in hearts transformed by the sovereign grace of God. They are not activities that can be done or requirements that can be fulfilled by the depraved human heart.

Doing as Absolutely Necessary

So far in this chapter I have been defending my use of the word doing to describe what Acts 20:21 requires. Someone might reasonably ask, If doing is such a controversial word, why use it? Because of this reasonable question, let me conclude this chapter by insisting that it is necessary to speak of doing in some sense.

When the Philippian jailor cried out, What must I do to be saved? Paul did not reply: Don't talk about doing. Salvation is all of grace. There is nothing you can do. He told him that he had to do something to be saved. He told him to believe in the Lord Jesus Christ. Similarly in Acts 2:37 we read the following:

> Now when they heard this, they were pierced to the heart, and said to Peter and the rest of the apostles, "Brethren, what shall we do?" 38 Peter said to them, "Repent, and each of you be baptized in the name of Jesus Christ for the forgiveness of your sins; and you will receive the gift of the Holy Spirit.

Here again Peter does not rebuke their request to know what they should do. He tells them to do something. He tells them to repent.

The Bible speaks of "substitionary atonement," but it never speaks of "substitutionary repentance" or "substitutionary faith." Christ dies for us and in our place, but he does not believe or repent for us. Those are things that we must do if we are to experience God's salvation. That is why I must speak of the two things you must do to be saved. That is why you must speak of the two things you must do to be saved when you share the gospel.

CHAPTER 2:

ON BEING SAVED

I made clear in the last chapter that I do not assume that everyone who reads these pages has not been saved. But neither do I assume that everyone who reads these pages understands exactly what I mean by *being saved*. Since it is really important that all my readers understand this terminology, let me address for a few paragraphs what I mean by *being saved*.

Acts 20:21 presents repentance and faith as matters of solemn importance:

> ...solemnly testifying to both Jews and Greeks of repentance toward God and faith in our Lord Jesus Christ

The reason for the solemn importance of repentance and faith resides in the fact that the people to whom Paul was "solemnly testifying" faith and repentance needed to *be saved*. But, again, what does that mean?

Generally speaking, when I refer to *being saved*, I mean to focus attention on the use of this word in the New Testament. The main Greek word for being saved (in its verb form) occurs 106 times in the New Testament. In order to understand how I am using it here, I must make a couple of distinctions.

When you look at how this word is used in the New Testament, it is clear that it is used to refer to two quite different kinds of salvation. It is used to refer to refer to salvation from sickness and death. Thus, it refers to what we might call physical or temporal salvation. It is used this way in Matthew 8:25; 9:21, 22; 14:30 and in Matthew 9:21-22 actually translated "made well." It is also, however, used to refer to salvation from our sins and the wrath of God against our sins. We may call this spiritual or eternal salvation. This is, of course, the meaning that lies behind my use of *be saved* in the title of this book.

The very first use of this word in the New Testament illustrates the spiritual or eternal use of the word.

> **Matthew 1:21:** "She will bear a Son; and you shall call His name Jesus, for He will save His people from their sins."

"Jesus" derives from a Hebrew word that means savior. Christ is named *savior* because "He will save His people." Notice, however, that He does not save them from their sicknesses or even from physical death, but "from their sins."

But what does the Bible mean by saying that Jesus saves His people from their sins? It is true that Jesus saves His people from being practically dominated by the enslaving power of sinful habits. It is gloriously true that gradually, but powerfully and irresistibly He saves them from the spiritual power of sin. This process begins with the repentance toward God which we will study a little later in this book.

All this is wonderfully true. Yet the most basic thing the Bible means when it speaks of Jesus saving us from sin is that we are saved from the penalty of sin. We are saved, in other words, from the wrath of God against our sins. The worst and most basic evil which our sin creates is the wrath of God against us. This wrath is threatened against the world of sinners. It is only through Christ's salvation that we are delivered from it.

> **Romans 5:9-10:** Much more then, having now been justified by His blood, we shall be saved from the wrath *of God* through Him. For if while we were enemies we were reconciled to God through the death of His Son, much more, having been reconciled, we shall be saved by His life.

> **1 Thessalonians 5:9:** For God has not destined us for wrath, but for obtaining salvation through our Lord Jesus Christ,

How does Jesus save His people from the wrath of God against their sin? He does it—as Romans 5:9-10 says—by His blood and by His death. His blood and death reconcile them to God and justify them in God's sight. That is to say, Jesus suffers in their place the wrath their sins deserved. He is their substitutionary curse-bearer. In this way God's wrath toward them is appeased, placated, or calmed. Thus, they are saved from His wrath and stand not guilty and positively righteous before His holy judgment seat.

Now with regard to this kind of salvation—being saved from our sins and God's wrath—another distinction is necessary to understand exactly what I mean by being saved. The New Testament teaches that the salvation of the one who believes in Christ has three tenses: past, present, and future. That is, he has been saved. He is being saved. He will be saved. Let me explain.

The believer in Christ has been saved—past tense. In other words a person is saved when he initially believes in Jesus Christ. This initial event in which one becomes a Christian is called *being saved* in the Bible. Here are some clear examples:

> **Acts 2:47:** praising God and having favor with all the people. And the Lord was adding to their number day by day those who were being saved.
>
> **Romans 8:24:** For in hope we have been saved, but hope that is seen is not hope; for who hopes for what he already sees?
>
> **1 Corinthians 1:21:** For since in the wisdom of God the world through its wisdom did not come to know God, God was well-pleased through the foolishness of the message preached to save those who believe.
>
> **Ephesians 2:8:** For by grace you have been saved through faith; and that not of yourselves, it is the gift of God;
>
> **Titus 3:5:** He saved us, not on the basis of deeds which we have done in righteousness, but according to His mercy, by the washing of regeneration and renewing by the Holy Spirit,

The New Testament also teaches that the Christian is in the process of being saved—present tense. This aspect or tense of salvation probably has reference to the present and ongoing work of Christ in which the believer is preserved in the grace of God and in which the power of sin over him in his practical life is more and more broken. This is an emphasis frequently overlooked in our day. Here are some examples of this emphasis.

1 Corinthians 1:18: For the word of the cross is foolishness to those who are perishing, but to us who are being saved it is the power of God.

2 Corinthians 2:15: For we are a fragrance of Christ to God among those who are being saved and among those who are perishing;

2 Timothy 4:18: The Lord will rescue me from every evil deed, and will bring me safely to His heavenly kingdom; to Him be the glory forever and ever. Amen.

Finally, the New Testament teaches that the believer will be saved—future tense. This refers to the salvation or eternal life he will receive when Christ returns. In that day he will be saved from the condemnation which the world of sinners will experience in the Day of Judgment. This also is an emphasis frequently overlooked in our day. Notice the following passages.

Matthew 10:22: "You will be hated by all because of My name, but it is the one who has endured to the end who will be saved."

Matthew 24:13: "But the one who endures to the end, he will be saved."

1 Corinthians 3:15: If any man's work is burned up, he will suffer loss; but he himself will be saved, yet so as through fire.

1 Corinthians 5:5 to deliver such a one to Satan for the destruction of his flesh, so that his spirit may be saved in the day of the Lord Jesus.

Thus, each of the three tenses of salvation is a legitimate way to speak of the Christian's salvation. In this book and in the title to this book, however, I am limiting the reference of *being saved* to that salvation which is past for every true believer. Every true believer in Christ has been saved. That is what I mean by *being saved* here. I refer to what it takes to become a Christian. I mean what you have to do to pass out of a condition in which you are under the wrath of God and into a condition in which you are under His saving grace and favor. I am not talking about all the things that may be necessary to do in order to endure to the end (though I am persuaded that all those things are simply the fruit and extension of faith and repentance.) I am talking simply about those things which are involved in the initial event of *being saved*.

Though I am writing this book primarily as a Bible study for evangelists rather than an evangelistic Bible study, I will ask you at the end of this book if you have been saved. Because the first thing you need in order to be an evangelist is to be saved yourself, I will press on you the question, *Have you done the two things you must do to be saved?* When I do, I will be referring to the initial but full salvation which comes when one exercises repentance toward God and faith toward our Lord Jesus Christ. Please remember that when I speak of being saved in this book I mean this initial salvation. Otherwise you may misapply what I am saying to another dimension of salvation and misunderstand what I am teaching.

CHAPTER 3:

ON THE RELATION OF REPENTANCE AND FAITH

This chapter and the next take up another preliminary issue in relation to faith and repentance. This issue is at the bottom of all sorts of questions that may be raised about God requiring two things to be saved. Are both repentance and faith really crucial to being saved? Do we need both to be saved? Does God require both universally? Do all men need both to repent and to believe? Are repentance and faith inseparable? Can we have one of them without the other? Assuming that we cannot, is it possible that repentance and faith are just two names for the same thing—and not *two* things at all?

All these important questions are clearly answered by a careful study of Acts 20:21 in its New Testament context. My method in approaching this verse will be to study carefully its contents on its own, but also to bring to bear on its meaning every passage in the New Testament where the key terms for repentance and faith occur significantly close to each other. In the exposition of this passage we will look at every passage in which repentance and faith occur either in the same verse or within a couple of verses of one another. Our goal is to clearly understand the relation of repentance and faith to one another and answer the questions this naturally raises.

Let me preview for you my response to the question of the relationship of repentance and faith. This relationship can be summarized in four key words.

> *They are both **crucial**.*
> *They are both **universal**.*
> *They are both **inseparable**.*
> *But they are **distinguishable**.*

They are both crucial.

The crucial character of the faith and repentance mentioned here is made clear by a number of things.

The meaning of the words, "solemnly testify," indicate how crucial repentance and faith are.

The importance and necessity of both these graces is declared by the opening words of the verse. Paul tells us that he solemnly testified of these things. This is an unusually strong word. Greek dictionaries give definitions like the following: *solemnly witness, bear witness (to), testify (about), give a solemn warning, admonish, earnestly ask, strongly tell, strongly urge, insist, declare solemnly and emphatically, charge under solemn oath, warn.*

The first two occurrences of this word in the New Testament clearly illustrate the meaning, solemnity, and emphasis of the Greek word.

> **Luke 16:28:** for I have five brothers— that he may warn them, lest they also come to this place of torment. '

Here the word, solemnly testify, is translated *warn*. The rich man who is in hell wants Abraham to send someone to solemnly testify to them about the danger they are in of going to hell. This is solemn indeed!

> **Acts 2:40:** And with many other words he solemnly testified and kept on exhorting them, saying, "Be saved from this perverse generation!"

In this verse Peter is responding to the Jewish crowd which asked him how they could escape condemnation for murdering the Messiah. This is certainly a solemn matter. Thus, Luke describes Peter as *solemnly testifying* about it to the Jews.

Secondly, the use of solemnly testify in this very passage shows how crucial faith and repentance are.

Twice in this very passage this very, same word is used. It is used first to describe the solemn testimony of certain New Testament prophets that Paul would suffer when he arrived in Jerusalem.

Acts 20:23: except that the Holy Spirit ***solemnly testifies*** to me in every city, saying that bonds and afflictions await me.

It is the second use of this word that is most important to show how crucial faith and repentance are. It is used in...

Acts 20:24: But I do not account my life of any value nor as precious to myself, if only I may accomplish my course and the ministry which I received from the Lord Jesus, to ***testify*** to the gospel of the grace of God.

Here Paul says that his ministry among them was to *solemnly testify* to the gospel of the grace of God. This is clearly parallel to verse 21 where Paul solemnly testifies to repentance toward God and faith toward our Lord Jesus Christ. The point is that what is called here the gospel of the grace of God is described in verse 21 as repentance toward God and faith in our Lord Jesus Christ. Testifying to these two graces was testifying to the gospel of the grace of God! We are preaching the gospel, and we are preaching grace, when we preach repentance toward God and faith toward the Lord Jesus Christ!

In the third place parallel passages where faith and repentance are used together in the same verse show how crucial repentance and faith are.

There are four passages in the New Testament where the Greek roots for repentance and faith are used together in the same passage. One of them is Acts 20:21. Each of the other three emphasizes the crucial or critical importance of these two graces in different ways.

The first is Mark 1:15.

Mark 1:15 and saying, "The time is fulfilled, and the kingdom of God is at hand; repent and believe in the gospel."

Here we learn that when Jesus began His ministry after His baptism and temptation He required two responses to the gospel He preached.

He commanded men to repent and believe the gospel. Both are part of the *initial* gospel preaching of Jesus. Both are *evangelical* graces, that is, required responses to the gospel.

The second of these passages is Acts 19:4.

> **Acts 19:4** And Paul said, "John baptized with the baptism of repentance, telling the people to believe in Him who was coming after him, that is, in Jesus."

Here we learn that both repentance and faith were part of the preaching of the forerunner of Jesus. Part of the message of repentance, was telling people to believe in Jesus. Part of the requirement for baptism was by implication believing in the coming Messiah, Jesus. This is probably why Paul baptized these disciples here again. If they were ignorant of the teaching about Jesus the Messiah, their baptism of repentance was defective. Both repentance and faith are *original* parts of John's gospel.

The third and final of these passages is Hebrews 6:1.

> **Hebrews 6:1:** Therefore leaving the elementary teaching about the Christ, let us press on to maturity, not laying again a foundation of repentance from dead works and of faith toward God,

Here repentance and faith are described as two of the six foundations of Christian teaching. Hebrews 5:12 in the near context describes these two things as "elementary principles" of Christianity. Both are *foundational* issues of the Christian life.

These parallel passages have constrained us to describe these two graces with several important modifiers. They are initial, evangelical, original, and foundational requirements of the gospel. Thus, they must be described as the two things you must do to be saved.

But important as all of what we have looked at is, I have still to set before you those passages which make most clear the fact that repentance and faith are crucial to becoming a Christian.

There are in the fourth place a number of passages in the Book of Acts where each distinctly is required for salvation.

There is no more important question than, "What must I do to be saved?" Yet, the Bible appears to give and in some sense does give two different replies to this question. Peter in Acts 2:37, 38 when asked by the Jews what they must do be saved tells them to repent.

> **Acts 2:37-38:** Now when they heard *this,* they were pierced to the heart, and said to Peter and the rest of the apostles, "Brethren, what shall we do?" Peter *said* to them, "Repent, and each of you be baptized in the name of Jesus Christ for the forgiveness of your sins; and you will receive the gift of the Holy Spirit.

Paul in Acts 16:30, 31 tells the Philippian jailer to believe when he asks the same question.

> **Acts 16:30-31:** and after he brought them out, he said, "Sirs, what must I do to be saved?" They said, "Believe in the Lord Jesus, and you will be saved, you and your household."

So what is the answer to the question, "What must I do to be saved?" Is it "repent" or "believe" or both? The book of Acts is a prime example of the Bible's two answers to that question. For the answer, "repent," note Acts 3:19; 5:31; 11:18; 17:30. For the answer, "believe," note Acts 8:12, 13; 10:43; 11:17; 13:39.

Many issues are raised by a comparison of these passages with one another. If the answer to the question, *What must I do to be saved?* is "repent," why does the Bible only say believe in certain places? If the answer is believe, why does the Bible only mention repentance in some places? If both are necessary, why aren't both always mentioned? Such perplexing issues are important and deserve good answers. I will attempt to provide answers to them below. Yet at least one thing is clear. Both repentance and faith are crucial to being saved. They are the two things you must do to be saved.

Before I proceed any further, I must stop to press what I have just said. The gospel of the grace of God is not just about what God will do. It is also about what you must do. The answer to the question, What must I do to be saved? is not: *You can do nothing. Salvation is all of grace*. Salvation is all of grace, but there is something—actually some *things*—you must do to be saved. If you do these things, salvation is still all of grace. But even though salvation remains all of grace, still you must do these two things. The Bible says that you yourself personally must repent and believe the gospel! Do not plead, and do not allow others to plead, inability to repent and believe. Such inability is rooted in a deep unwillingness and stubborn refusal to repent and believe. It is motivated by a terrible dislike of repentance and faith for which sinners are completely accountable.

On the other hand, you may be reading this and wants to be saved. If you are willing to repent and believe, nothing stands between you and salvation. You may—you must—right now repent of your sins and entrust yourself to Christ's salvation!

Unhelpful deductions have often been drawn from the biblical doctrine of the total inability of sinners to respond to the gospel. Such total inability does not change what the gospel requires or change what we should tell sinners to do to be saved. Some have reasoned that, since men cannot believe and repent, we should give some other advice to men when we preach the gospel. But there is no other helpful advice to give sinful men except gospel advice. That advice is to repent and believe the gospel. If, therefore, someone asks you what he must do to be saved, do not tell them that they can only pray for a new heart. Do not tell them that they must wait on God. Do not tell them that they can do nothing. Praying for a new heart or waiting on God *impenitently and unbelievingly* will do no one any good. (Assumedly, if someone is willing to pray for a new heart, they should be willing to repent and believe. If they are not willing to repent and believe the gospel, telling them to pray for a new heart will do nothing but confuse the gospel call.) We must rather tell people what the Bible tells them to do to be saved: *Repent and believe the gospel!*

CHAPTER 4:

ON THE RELATION OF REPENTANCE AND FAITH (CONTINUED)

We are in the middle of a preliminary study of Acts 20:21 in its New Testament context. Our goal is to clearly understand the relation of repentance and faith to one another and answer the questions about this relationship which naturally occur to people interested in being saved and also to people interested in telling other people how to be saved. In the last chapter I said that this relationship between faith and repentance can be summarized in four key words.

They are both ***crucial****.*
They are both ***universal****.*
They are both ***inseparable****.*
But they are ***distinguishable****.*

Having seen the clear biblical witness to the crucial character of both faith and repentance, let me in this chapter take up the last three of the above points.

They are both universal.

When I say that faith and repentance are both *universal*, what do I mean? I mean that both repentance and faith are universally required of everyone in order to be saved!

This is clear in the first place from Acts 20:21 itself.

> **Acts 20:21:** solemnly testifying to both Jews and Greeks of repentance toward God and faith in our Lord Jesus Christ

Look at the text. Paul solemnly testified to "to *both Jews and Greeks* of repentance toward God and faith in our Lord Jesus Christ." This assertion that *both Jews and Greeks must both repent and believe* contradicts not a little superficial exposition of the Bible in our day. It has seemed to more than one "Bible teacher" that *repentance* was more appropriate to the Jews and the Old Testament and *faith* more appropriate to Gentiles and the New Testament. No such distinction is taught in the Bible. Several of the other texts where repentance and faith are mentioned in close proximity emphasize the universal demand of God for both of these graces in all those who would be saved.

One such passage is Acts 17:30-34.

> **Acts 17:30:** "Therefore having overlooked the times of ignorance, God is now declaring to men that all *people* everywhere should **repent** .... 34 But some men joined him and **believed**, among whom also were Dionysius the Areopagite and a woman named Damaris and others with them.

Do you see how repentance and faith are mentioned together here? Paul tells the Athenians gathered at the Areopagus that they must repent. They, therefore, believe. This is interesting and illuminating with regard to the relationship of faith and repentance. But my main point is that you should notice who is required to repent: *God is now declaring to men that all everywhere should repent.* Notice it is not just Jews who must repent. It is *all men everywhere*!

Another such passage is Acts 26:18-20. Notice the mention of faith in verse 18 and the reference to repentance in verse 20.

> **Acts 26:18:** to open their eyes so that they may turn from darkness to light and from the dominion of Satan to God, that they may receive forgiveness of sins and an inheritance among those who have been sanctified by **faith** in Me.' 19 "So, King Agrippa, I did not prove disobedient to the heavenly vision, 20 but *kept* declaring both to those of Damascus first, and *also* at Jerusalem and *then* throughout all the region of Judea, and *even* to the Gentiles, that they should **repent** and turn to God, performing deeds appropriate to repentance.

The extended description of those to whom Paul preached the necessity of both repentance and faith is emphatic. Verse 20 asserts that Paul "*kept* declaring both to those of Damascus first, and *also* at Jerusalem and *then* throughout all the region of Judea, and *even* to the Gentiles, that they should repent."

Repentance is not just for the Jews. Faith is not just for the Gentiles. Both are for everyone and required of everyone if they would be saved. All men are required both to repent and believe the gospel in order to be saved. We live in a day that is dizzy with Dispensational distinctions. But there is no Dispensational distinction to be made here. The way of salvation for every son of Adam and daughter of Eve has always been marked out since the beginning of the world by the demand for both repentance and faith.

They are both inseparable.

In our text repentance and faith are mentioned together: *repentance toward God and faith in our Lord Jesus Christ*. This fact reflects the reality that repentance and faith are inseparable graces. Under the heading *both are crucial* we saw that in four places these two graces of faith and repentance are mentioned together as crucial to being saved. Under *both are universal* we saw two passages (Acts 17 and 26) which assumed that *believing includes repentance* and *repentance includes believing*. Here I have only one more passage to mention—the only passage in the New Testament where faith and repentance are mentioned within two verses of the other that I have not yet shown you. It is Acts 11:17 and 18.

> **Acts 11:17:** "Therefore if God gave to them the same gift as *He gave* to us also after **believing** in the Lord Jesus Christ, who was I that I could stand in God's way?" 18 When they heard this, they quieted down and glorified God, saying, "Well then, God has granted to the Gentiles also the **repentance** *that leads* to life."

Do you see the conclusion that these Christians drew from Peter's testimony? Peter affirmed that the Gentiles had believed in the Lord Jesus. They concluded that they had repented.

Why? Had Paul said anything about their repenting? Not that we know of. Not that the text says. But these Christians knew what every Christian needs to know. Truly believing always involves and cannot be separated from truly repenting. Repentance unto life and saving faith cannot be separated.

But we must now come to a fourth and balancing point. Having seen that both faith and repentance are crucial, universal, and inseparable, we must see that they are distinguishable.

But they are distinguishable.

My point is simply this: *The fact that faith and repentance cannot be separated does not mean that they are the same thing.* They are, in other words, inseparable, but distinct.

But why must we be sure to understand this? It is because someone might conclude that *repentance and faith are just two different names for the same thing. They are synonyms.* This might appear to be a natural conclusion from what we have been saying. I am convinced, however, that the biblical data does not permit it.

In the first place, Acts 20:21 text teaches faith and repentance are different things. Acts 20:21 mentions faith and repentance as two different things. It underlines the distinction by emphasizing the fact that repentance and faith focus on different things. It reads: "repentance toward God and faith toward our Lord Jesus Christ." Did I misread the text? No, though the NASB reads *repentance toward God and faith in our Lord Jesus Christ*, the original is better translated as I did. Why? Because the preposition translated *toward* in *repentance toward God* is the same preposition in the Greek as the one translated *in* in the phrase *faith in our Lord Jesus Christ.* This is why some English translations (KJV, NKJV) translate the phrase exactly as I have read it to you.

This preposition has the basic idea of *into* or *toward*. Here it tells us that repentance and faith focus on or face toward different things. The idea is the same as if, supposing I were preaching to you, I said that from where I stand I am facing the congregation and that from where you sit you are facing me. Similarly, repentance and faith are directed toward different objects. Repentance focuses on God and His law. Faith focuses on Christ and His grace. Repentance and faith possess different roles in salvation. Faith highlights the grace that works the saving change. Repentance highlights the saving change that grace produces.

Furthermore, repentance and faith refer to different things. That is, they have and require two different definitions. Failing to distinguish them would run the danger of flattening the differences between them. This in turn might result in not understanding them with the clarity we must if, as it does, our salvation depends on it. In the rest of this book I will provide thorough studies, first, of the nature of repentance and, second, of the nature of saving faith that will make clear that they are different. But remember I am *not* saying they can be *separated*, I am only saying that *must* be *distinguished*. That brings me to an illustration which I hope will help you understand the inseparable, but distinct relationship of repentance and faith.

A Summarizing Illustration

A number of simple but important truths have become clear in this study. Both repentance and faith are necessary if anyone is to be saved. Everyone must both repent and believe the gospel. One or the other is not enough. Repentance and faith are inseparable. You can never have one without having the other. Yet, though they are inseparable, they are distinct or distinguishable.

Now I have an illustration of this. It may strike you as a little weird, but I think its helpfulness will make up for its weirdness. You know what Siamese twins are. They are twin babies born attached to each other in some part of their bodies. Let me introduce you to Siamese twins named Sam and Pam. They are joined at the heart. They have only one heart between them. They can never be separated without killing them both. Yet they are different. Sam is a boy and Pam is a girl. They have different names. Another strange thing about Sam and Pam is that they are joined at the back so they always face different directions. They are two different people, but they are always found together. One can never go anywhere without the other.

It is just so with repentance and faith. They are always found together. They are joined at the heart. They are, however, two different graces and focus on different things.

Closing Lesson and Its Applications:

Several vital practical applications flow from a right understanding of the relation of faith and repentance.

First, there can be no priority in time or logic assigned to faith or repentance as over against the other. People sometimes argue about whether repentance or faith comes first in the order of salvation. What is the answer in light of what we have said? Since they are inseparable, they always come together. People may at first experience more of one than the other, but every true Christian has both and experiences both. Sam or Pam may appear in the doorway first, but Sam is always right there behind the other.

Second, faith is a mark of true repentance. There is a sorrow for sin that is not true repentance. Judas had a sorrow for sin, but he went out, hanged himself, and went to hell. The problem with his repentance was that he could not believe that he could be forgiven. In the words of the old catechism, all true repentance must have or involve *an apprehension of the mercy of God in Christ*. The word *apprehension* means a real understanding or a deep grasp of God's mercy. True repentance involves a deep appreciation of the mercy of God in forgiving sins. It involves an ability to apply this mercy to our own sins. You do not have (and no one has) true repentance if you are unable to believe the forgiveness of your own sins through the mercy of God in Christ. Do you know anything of such repentance?

Third, repentance is a mark of saving faith. In our day there are many who profess faith in Christ, but show no true repentance in their life. Faith has been so diluted and watered down that it has become no more than a momentary decision for Christ expressed perhaps in a raised hand, the walking of an aisle, or a few tears. True faith, however, grows out of a deep sense of sin and results in a new commitment to Christ as Lord. This requires a turning from sin in one's life. If you have truly come to Christ, you have repented of habitually living in defiance of His laws.

Fourth, a balanced emphasis on these two gospel duties must be maintained, if one or both of these graces are not to be perverted. We must never give up preaching the one for the sake of the other. Even though we may feel strongly that one or the other is *the missing note* in today's church, we must continue to preach both. Sam without Pam is not really Sam, and Pam without Sam is not really Pam!

Fifth, the most appropriate truth must be stressed in any given situation. In Galatians speaking against the legalistic Judaizers,

Paul said very little about repentance. He rather stressed justification by faith alone. To the idolatrous Gentiles in Athens a different emphasis appears. Paul addressed to them the command that all men everywhere should repent.

It is my opinion that in our day most of our countrymen and fellow churchmen need a message of repentance. But we must not over-react so that our children and churches never hear the message of free grace and justification by faith alone.

Conclusion

What are the two things you must do to be saved? I hope you can now answer that all-important question with confidence. Now you are in a position with judgment day honesty to consider another question. Have you done the two things you must do to be saved? However you answer that question, you are also ready to go a little deeper in your understanding of repentance toward God and faith toward our Lord Jesus Christ.

CHAPTER 5:

ON THE TREE OF REPENTANCE

The first of the two things each one of us needs to be saved is according to Acts 20:21 *repentance toward God*. Over the next several chapters I want to explore the tree of repentance with some care. The danger with such detail and thoroughness is that (as the old saying goes) we will miss the whole tree in focusing on its details. My goal in this chapter is, therefore, to look at the tree as a whole.

The illustration of the tree of repentance I mentioned above likens repentance to a fruit tree. I think this illustration (which I will use throughout the part of this book on repentance) is really helpful in tying this subject together. So I want you to think with me about the tree of repentance.

The illustration which likens repentance to a tree is not original with me. (Little in this book is.) I first heard it used in preaching on repentance several decades ago. I am fairly certain that it was not original with the fine preacher that I heard use it. I have embellished it just a little, but I want to be sure everyone knows that I do not claim that this helpful illustration is my own. I owe it to the influence of others.

The Fruit of Repentance

It is probably the fact that repentance is said frequently and specifically to have fruit that suggests the analogy of a tree. Here are the key passages:

> **Matthew 3:8:** "Therefore ***bring forth fruit in keeping with repentance***;

> **Luke 3:8:** "Therefore ***bring forth fruits in keeping with repentance***, and do not begin to say to yourselves, 'We have Abraham for our father,' for I say to you that God is able from these stones to raise up children to Abraham.

> **Acts 26:20:** but *kept* declaring both to those of Damascus first, and *also* at Jerusalem and *then* throughout all the region of Judea, and *even* to the Gentiles, that they should repent and turn to God, ***performing deeds appropriate to repentance***.

The key things about the fruit of repentance are three. First, the fruit consists in good deeds of service to God. Second, this fruit is the evidence that repentance is genuine and not fake or superficial. Third, the fruit of repentance must not be confused with repentance itself. The fruit must not be confused with the root (or the trunk and branches)! Repentance is a matter of the heart. Fruit is, at least in part, a matter of the hand.

The Foliage (or Leaves) of Repentance

In an astonishing amount of places the New Testament associates baptism with repentance. Baptism is even described as the baptism of repentance.

> **Luke 3:3** And he c:ame into all the district around the Jordan, preaching a **baptism** of **repentance** for the forgiveness of sins...

I liken baptism to the foliage or leaves on the tree of repentance because like the leaves or foliage on a tree baptism is a sign of life. That is, in the gospel age baptism is the religious rite which says that a person has repented and has new life. It is Jesus' will even today that one who truly repents show this in baptism, just as leaves show that a tree is alive.

The Trunk and Branches of Repentance

Just as the trunk and branches are the heart of a tree, so in my illustration the trunk and branches represent the heart or essence of true repentance. The first use of the word, repentance, in the New Testament is Matthew 3:8: "Therefore bear fruit in keeping with repentance." The word translated, repentance, in this verse is the main word for repentance in the New Testament. It is built around a root that refers to the mind or heart. It literally means a "change of mind." At least two important things about this word will be stressed. First, it is important to emphasize that repentance is not essentially an outward action. Repentance is not *penance*. It is first and foremost a matter of the heart. Second, it is important to stress that this change of mind is not light or superficial. The mind in the Bible controls the man, and a change of mind radically, though progressively, changes the man from the inside out!

The Roots of Repentance

Such a change of mind does not emerge in a vacuum. Like the song from the musical says, *Nothing comes from nothing, nothing ever could!* Even so the tree of repentance has roots. That is to say, it grows out of two fundamental alterations at the bottom of a man's soul.

It grows up from a fundamental alteration with regard to the matter of sin. This alteration consists in a new sorrow for sin. Perhaps the key passage on repentance growing out of sorrow and regret for sin is the following:

> 2 Corinthians 7:8-11: For though I caused you sorrow by my letter, I do not regret it; though I did regret it—*for* I see that that letter caused you sorrow, though only for a while. I now rejoice, not that you were made sorrowful, but that you were made sorrowful to *the point of* repentance; for you were made sorrowful according to *the will of* God, so that you might not suffer loss in anything through us. For the sorrow that is according to *the will of* God produces a repentance without regret, *leading* to salvation, but the sorrow of the world produces death. For behold what earnestness this very thing, this godly sorrow, has produced in you: what vindication of yourselves, what indignation, what fear, what longing, what zeal, what avenging of wrong! In everything you demonstrated yourselves to be innocent in the matter.

But sorrow for sin by itself is not sufficient to produce true repentance. Repentance also requires a personal grasp that one may be forgiven of sin. This conviction that "there is forgiveness with God that He may be feared" (Psa. 130:4) must emerge in the bottom of a man's soul. There must be a spark of conviction that "if I repent, my sins will be forgiven." Without this, conviction of sin and even sorrow for sin will never culminate or grow up in the tree of true repentance.

This is why Luke 24:47 speaks of the fact that repentance is for the forgiveness of sins. In other words people actually repent only if they believe this will lead to their forgiveness.

> that repentance ***for forgiveness of sins*** should be proclaimed in His name to all the nations, beginning from Jerusalem.

The Soil of Repentance

In speaking of the soil of repentance I am asking this simple question: In what kind of soil will such a tree grow? I will show that the biblical answer to this question begins with the realization that such a tree will not grow in the natural soil of the human heart. The biblical answer is only fully appreciated when we realize that repentance can only grow in a heart plowed up and fertilized by God's sovereign grace. That is why Paul ascribes repentance to the sovereign working of God.

> 2 Timothy 2:25: with gentleness correcting those who are in opposition, if perhaps God may grant them repentance leading to the knowledge of the truth

Conclusion

In the above five analogies the illustration of the tree of repentance may be understood. Through them I hope each of my readers will be able to answer the question, *Is the tree of repentance planted in my life?* I also hope you will be explain to others more clearly how they can know if they have repentance toward God in their hearts and lives.

CHAPTER 6:

ON THE SOIL OF REPENTANCE

The soil of the fruit tree of repentance is the sovereign grace of God. That is to say, true repentance toward God only grows in a heart and life transformed by God's special, effectual, irresistible calling and grace. To put this in other words, repentance is the gift of God. The Bible teaches that there is an outward call of the gospel which comes to all who hear it. It is of this of which Jesus speaks when He says in Matthew 22:14, "many are called, but few *are* chosen." Not all of those called outwardly by the gospel are saved. But the same verse teaches that some of those called are "chosen." Elsewhere the Bible confines the *inward* or *effectual* call of God to those who are chosen.

> **Romans 8:30:** And these whom He predestined, He also called; and these whom He called, He also justified; and these whom He justified, He also glorified.

> **1 Corinthians 1:23-24:** but we preach Christ crucified, to Jews a stumbling block and to Gentiles foolishness, but to those who are the called, both Jews and Greeks, Christ the power of God and the wisdom of God.

> **2 Timothy 1:** who has saved us and called us with a holy calling, not according to our works, but according to His own purpose and grace which was granted us in Christ Jesus from all eternity

This is why we must distinguish between the outward call of the gospel and the effectual call of the gospel which actually saves people. It is this effectual call which transforms the soil of the human heart. It is this call which grants the gift of repentance to sinners.

The Bible says that in the mouth of two or three witnesses every fact should be confirmed. There are actually many more than three texts that teach that repentance is a gift of God, but there are three texts in the New Testament that explicitly use the word, repentance and assert that it is the gift of God. Please consider them with me one at a time.

The first such text is Acts 5:31:

> **Acts 5:31:** "He is the one whom God exalted to His right hand as a Prince and a Savior, to grant repentance to Israel, and forgiveness of sins..."

Little comment is needed to see the teaching of this text. It teaches that Jesus has been exalted to the right hand of God. From that exalted and powerful position He is able to grant repentance to Israel and by implication to men He chooses from any other nation. The fact that Jesus can also give the gift of repentance to Gentiles is actually the thrust of the next text.

The second text is Acts 11:18:

> **Acts 11:18:** And when they heard this, they quieted down, and glorified God, saying, "Well then, God has granted to the Gentiles also the repentance *that leads* to life."

When the Jewish believers received the report of how the household of Cornelius had believed and received the gift of the Holy Spirit, they submitted to God's providence. They concluded that the faith of the Gentiles and their reception of gift of the Spirit must be the result of God through the exalted Jesus sovereignly granting them repentance.

The third text is 2 Timothy 2:25:

> **2 Timothy 2:25:** with gentleness correcting those who are in opposition, if perhaps God may grant them repentance leading to the knowledge of the truth,

Often the teaching of the Bible about God's sovereign grace is diluted and distorted. The way this sometimes happens is that, while it is admitted that God gives men the gift of repentance, it is then added that God gives this gift to everyone. They then go on to say that it is up to men with their free will to either accept or reject this gift of repentance.

There is much wrong with this interpretation. For instance, it contradicts the idea taught clearly in the passages we saw above that there is a special effectual calling which comes only to those chosen. 2 Timothy 2:25, however, contains an explicit rebuttal of this interpretation. Notice that Paul is uncertain if God will give repentance to those who are in opposition. Thus, he says, "if perhaps God may grant them repentance." If God gives this repentance to everyone, why does Paul express this doubt? Paul certainly should not have qualified his statement this way if the fact is that God gives repentance to everyone who hears the gospel if they will just take the gift. But Paul says *if perhaps* because he knows that as a matter of fact, God does not give repentance to everyone, but only to those He chooses.

What is the practical value of understanding that true repentance is a gift of God's sovereign, electing grace?

First, it demonstrates that repentance is consistent with grace alone for salvation. Many in our day have very imbalanced understandings of grace and the gospel because of the teaching they have received. This imbalance causes them to fear that making repentance one of the two things you must do to be saved is teaching a kind of works-salvation. In other words, they think that repentance is a kind of work we do to save ourselves. Thus, they reject the idea that repentance is necessary to salvation. This conclusion ought never to be entertained. One (though not the only) reason why it should not be entertained is that repentance itself is the gift of God's grace. How can repentance be a kind of work which earns salvation, when it is itself the gift of free grace?

Second, it prevents reducing the demands of biblical repentance down to the level of the natural man. There is a tendency in our day to make results the only thing that matters in evangelism. Of course, we ought to want genuine results and genuine conversions from our preaching. But some people become so caught up in this that they are tempted to reduce the demands of the gospel to "get results." That is, they dilute the gospel to the point where (they think) that the natural man will swallow it.

They reason this way, *If I tell the natural man that he must actually repent and turn to God in order to bring forth fruit and serve God and live a godly life, he won't want to do that. What unsaved man would do that? If I am to get a decision, I must not ask that of him. If I do, he will never respond.* With this kind of reasoning they subtly dilute the demands of repentance to the point where they are no longer distasteful to the natural man.

The truth that the soil of the tree of repentance is the sovereign grace of God helps us resist this temptation. If we understand that no man will ever genuinely repent without the grace of God changing his heart, then we will not feel that we have to dilute the demands of the gospel. We will put our confidence in God. We will remember that, if God is displeased with us, He will not bless us. We will simply give the water of life to the sinner in its undiluted strength, believing that if he is one of God's chosen God will help him drink it.

Third, this teaching about the soil of repentance should give hope to the sinner who is truly aware of how desperate his condition is. Perhaps someone is reading these pages who has caught a glimpse of how desperately wicked he is. You feel deeply your heart's aversion to all that is good and holy. You feel deeply your lack of love for the Lord Jesus Christ. There is hope for you. There is a God who changes the soil of hearts so that the tree of true repentance can grow in them. He can do this for you. In fact, the reality that you have caught a glimpse of your wickedness may itself be an indication that He is doing this for you. A feeling sense of sin is one root of true repentance.

Fourth, this study of the soil of true repentance shows us who should be thanked and glorified for repentance. Can you imagine what it would be like if repentance were not the gift of God? Suppose that one man repented because he was better than another was. Can you imagine how arrogant Christians would be? They could say, Did I not make myself to differ by repenting when the other guy was not smart enough or spiritual enough or humble enough to repent?

Repentance being the gift of God destroys all such boasting. The natural effect of teaching that repentance is the gift of God is to give all glory to God and to lead us to glorify, adore, and worship him for the repentance that by His sovereign choice He granted to us and to others. It will make us thank Him for making us to differ. Not just for the blessings of creation, but for the sovereign grace of salvation, we will sing the doxology to God.

> Praise God from Whom all blessings flow
> Praise Him all creatures here below
> Praise Him above ye heavenly hosts
> Praise Father, Son, and Holy Ghost!

Or we might apply to ourselves the words of this great old hymn.

> Why was I made to hear Thy voice and enter while there's room
> When thousands make a wretched choice and rather starve than come
> Twas the same love that spread the feat that sweetly drew us in
> Else we had still refused to taste and perished in our sin.

CHAPTER 7:

ON THE ROOTS OF REPENTANCE

The fruit tree of repentance has two main roots from which it draws its life and nourishment. The Westminster Shorter Catechism describes them as *a true sense of sin and apprehension of the mercy of God in Christ.*

The First Root—A True Sense of Sin

The true sense of sin of which the catechism speaks involves a sense of sorrow and remorse for sin. There are three major words for repentance used in the New Testament. The first and most important refers to it as a *change of mind* and heart about our sins. The second refers to it as a *turning* from our sin to God. The third refers to it as *remorse* or sorrow. It is this word I want you to think about for a moment. It is used in . . .

> **Matthew 21:30:** "And he came to the second and said the same thing. But he answered and said, 'I will not'; *yet* he afterward ***regretted*** *it* and went..."

In one important passage this sense of sorrow for sin is clearly brought out.

> **2 Corinthians 7:9:** I now rejoice, not that you were made sorrowful, but that you were made sorrowful to *the point of* repentance; for ***you were made sorrowful according to the will of God***, in order that you might not suffer loss in anything through us.10 For the sorrow that is according to *the will of* God produces a repentance without regret, *leading* to salvation; but the sorrow of the world produces death.

Another way in which this root of repentance in a true sense of sin is made clear is in the emphasis of the New Testament that it is *sinners* who must repent.

> **Luke 5:32:** "I have not come to call the righteous but sinners to repentance."

> **Luke 15:7:** "I tell you that in the same way, there will be *more* joy in heaven over one sinner who repents, than over ninety-nine righteous persons who need no repentance.

> **Luke 15:10:** "In the same way, I tell you, there is joy in the presence of the angels of God over one sinner who repents."

Clearly, the *sinners* mentioned in these passages are sinners who feel or have a sense of their sin. Jesus certainly does not mean to say that there are righteous men who are not sinners and who need not repent. He does mean to say that there are some men who wrongly think of themselves as righteous. This is clear from the analogy Jesus gives for repentance in the verse immediately preceding Luke 5:32. Only those who know they are sick go to a doctor. Only those who know they are sinners feel a need to repent.

> **Luke 5:31:** And Jesus answered and said to them, "*It is* not those who are well who need a physician, but those who are sick.

It is only when a man ceases to regard himself as deserving, righteous, and clean in the sight of God and begins to regard himself as undeserving, unrighteous, and unclean that there is found in him the seed of true repentance. You must be a sinner in order to repent. This is the reason perhaps that some of you have never repented. It is because you view yourself as never really having done anything very bad. You have never really come to view yourself as a sinner. It is only sinners who repent and only the ungodly (Romans 4:5) who are justified. You will not repent until you take your position as an ungodly sinner. Then, and only then, will you have that true sense of sin in which genuine repentance is rooted. Oh, please see yourself for what you are and admit you are a filthy sinner ... so that you can repent. The work of God only begins in someone's heart when he conceives a true sense of his sinfulness. It is a fearful and dreadful thing when a child, teen, or adult will not and cannot see, admit, and sense their sin. Why? In such a state they cannot repent and be forgiven!

But a word of caution is necessary here. Sometimes having a sense of one's sin has been stressed in such a way as to make sensitive souls wonder if they feel their sins sufficiently. They ask themselves, *Do I have enough conviction of sin? Is my sense of sin deep enough?*

Jesus suggests the answer to such scrupulous questions by the analogy of sickness He uses in Luke 5:31. To ask if you have enough conviction of sin is like asking how sick do I have to feel? What is the answer? You simply have to feel sick enough to go to a doctor! Similarly, when someone asks if they have enough sense or conviction of sin, the answer to their question is simply that they have to have enough to go to the great physician. If their sense of sin makes them want to go to the spiritual doctor, Jesus, then they have enough! If your sense of sin is sufficient to make you want to go to Christ, you have enough. The point of a conviction and sense of sin from God's point of view is not to torture us, but to save us by leading us to Christ. You need enough sense of the evil of sin to make you want Christ.

The old hymn asks the Holy Spirit to "convince us of our sins, then lead to Jesus' blood." The purpose of the conviction of sin is to lead us to Jesus' blood. When it has done that for you, you have enough sense of sin.

The Second Root—An Apprehension of God's Mercy in Christ

The second root main root of true repentance is according to the catechism *an apprehension of God's mercy in* Christ. The key word (and the most difficult word) in this phrase is *apprehension*. Synonyms for the way the catechism uses this word are perceive, grasp, and understand. The force of this word is to tell us that we need to understand and take hold of personally and practically God's mercy in Christ. Apprehension happens when someone sees and grasps a hammer with the intention of driving a nail with it. So we must see and grasp the promises of the gospel with the intention of applying them to ourselves.

In an earlier chapter I said that one thing we can learn from the fact that faith and repentance are inseparable is that all true repentance is believing repentance. Faith is one distinguishing mark of true repentance. Judas experienced remorse—a kind of repentance—but he did not have the faith to believe that he could be forgiven.

One of the major emphases of the New Testament is that people repent in order to be saved and in order to escape divine punishment. I hope this does not seem carnal or unspiritual to you. It should not. Doing what is right is never opposed to our truest and highest self-interest. God has built a natural self-love into human beings. He never calls upon us to act in a way that is truly contrary to an enlightened self-love. There is a selfish love that leads me to love myself instead of God and others. True self-love is always consistent with loving God most of all and loving our neighbor as ourselves.

Thus, repentance throughout the New Testament is motivated by a desire to experience God's salvation and escape God's wrath. In other words, there is in true repentance a confidence that, if I repent and turn to God, I will receive salvation. There is, in yet other words, a confidence or faith that it will do me some good to repent. Judas felt remorse, but he did not repent because he despaired. True repentance believes God's promise and turns to God with an apprehension of the mercy of God in Christ. True repentance lays hold of God's promises and is motivated to repent.

The evidence for this focuses our attention on one of the major emphases of the New Testament with regard to repentance. I have placed in bold the parts of the following verses which emphasize the reason people repent.

> **Matthew 3:7:** But when he saw many of the Pharisees and Sadducees coming for baptism, he said to them, "You brood of vipers, who warned you to ***flee from the wrath to come***?

> **Mark 1:4:** John the Baptist appeared in the wilderness preaching a baptism of repentance ***for the forgiveness of sins***.

> **Luke 3:3:** And he came into all the district around the Jordan,

preaching a baptism of repentance ***for the forgiveness of sins***...

Luke 24:47: and that repentance ***for forgiveness of sins*** should be proclaimed in His name to all the nations, beginning from Jerusalem.

Acts 5:31: "He is the one whom God exalted to His right hand as a Prince and a Savior, to grant repentance to Israel, ***and forgiveness of sins***.

Acts 11:18: And when they heard this, they quieted down, and glorified God, saying, "Well then, God has granted to the Gentiles also ***the repentance that leads to life***."

2 Peter 3:9: The Lord is not slow about His promise, as some count slowness, but is patient toward you, not wishing for any ***to perish*** but for all to come to repentance.

Luke 13:3: "I tell you, no, but unless you repent, ***you will all likewise perish***.

Luke 13:5: "I tell you, no, but unless you repent, ***you will all likewise perish***."

Luke 16:27: "And he said, 'Then I beg you, Father, that you send him to my father's house [28] for I have five brothers that he may warn them, lest they also come to ***this place of torment***. ' [29] "But Abraham *said, 'They have Moses and the Prophets; let them hear them.' [30] "But he said, 'No, Father Abraham, but if someone goes to them from the dead, they will repent!' "But he said to him, 'If they do not listen to Moses and the Prophets, neither will they be persuaded if someone rises from the dead.'"

One of the essential things necessary to convince people to repent is to convince them that it will do some good to repent. Visualize it this way. There you are. God's wrath is coming. A place of terrible torment awaits you. You are going to perish. Will you just sit there and do nothing about it? No, you must repent! There in front of you is the forgiveness of sins and eternal life. If you repent, if you flee from your evil lifestyle, if you return to God, you will be forgiven and receive eternal life. This is God's promise. What will it cost you? It will cost you only giving up that life of sin that has not satisfied and cannot satisfy.

If you have never repented, may God give you faith to believe what you may escape, what you may have, what you may be, if you repent.

Christian, always give hope when you are speaking with those who are lost, whether your children or your friends and acquaintances. Of course, I do not mean that hope should be given if they stay where they are spiritually. But give them hope if they will repent. Urge them to repent. Let them know that it will do some good. Never in disgust or irritation give up on people. Always take a priestly role. Tell them that they can still repent. Tell them that God will still forgive.

CHAPTER 8:

ON THE TRUNK AND BRANCHES OF REPENTANCE

When I speak of the trunk and branches of the tree of repentance, I intend to identify the fundamental nature or essence of true repentance. Here I must immediately clear away a significant obstacle to understanding the real nature of repentance.

In the history of the church repentance has too often been equated with what people call "doing penance." For instance, one English translation of the Bible uses this phrase to translate the Greek word for *repent* in Luke 13:3-5.

> No, I say to you: but unless you shall do penance, you shall all likewise perish. Or those eighteen upon whom the tower fell in Siloe, and slew them: think you, that they also were debtors above all the men that dwelt in Jerusalem? No, I say to you; but except you do penance, you shall all likewise perish.

Identifying the ways in which translating repent as *do penance* falls short would be a lengthy study. Here I only want to point out one of the major deficiencies of identifying repentance as *doing penance*.

What do people mean by doing penance? Doing penance always involves some outward action that is supposed to display or embody a sorrow for our sins. The problem with this understanding of penance as repentance is that it makes repentance something mainly external or outward. While biblical repentance certainly has outward manifestations, fundamentally it is an inward matter of the heart. Repentance does not consist essentially in the outward action, but in the *inward* attitude. If this is forgotten, it is liable to distort the whole biblical doctrine of repentance and along with this the doctrine of salvation by grace and faith alone.

Why am I so confident that biblical repentance is fundamentally an inward matter of the heart? It is simply because the main biblical word for repentance is *metanoia*. This word is derived from two Greek roots meaning *after* and *mind*. It means literally an "afterthought" or better yet a "change of mind." The word itself, therefore, speaks first and foremost of one's mind and heart and a change in one's mind and heart.

Here we must avoid another contemporary misunderstanding and misrepresentation of the nature of true repentance. In English when we speak of a change of mind or an afterthought, we may refer to something quite trivial like changing our mind from choosing steak for dinner at a restaurant to having chicken. Sad to say, some Christian teachers have thought and taught that repentance is not much different or deeper than some such trivial change of mind. They have said that repentance is simply a change of mind about Jesus. This change of mind, however, is merely a kind of mental gymnastics or intellectual exercise.

There is so much wrong with such teaching that it is hard even to know where to begin to refute it. But it is important to make clear its error, because this false view is widespread in our day. Allow me to list for you just a few of the reasons why it is so wrong.

First, according to the text on which this little book is based (Acts 20:21) the unique focus of repentance is on God. It is toward God, while faith is toward the Lord Jesus Christ. To make repentance merely a change of mind about Jesus is to confuse faith and repentance and to narrow the comprehensive alteration in one's thinking that repentance involves.

Second, we have already seen that repentance finds its roots in a true and experiential sense of and sorrow for sin and also in an apprehension of the mercy of God in Christ that makes us flee from the wrath to come. This is something more than a mere change of mind about the identity of Jesus. It is clearly a change that also involves radical changes in one's will and feelings, one's volitions and emotions.

Third, though repentance is fundamentally inward, in future chapters we will prove that all true repentance bears fruit and must bear fruit in a turning to God and doing works fitting for repentance. Such a change must be rooted in something more than a trivial change of mind about Jesus.

Fourth, changing your mind in the Bible is more than mental gymnastics or a change in one's surface intellectual opinions. The mind in Scripture is another way of referring to a man's soul. A man according to the biblical perspective is ruled by his mind. Here are three texts which say this in a way typical of the biblical perspective:

> **Romans 7:25:** I myself with my **mind** am serving the law of God.
>
> **Romans 12:2:** And do not be conformed to this world, but be transformed by the renewing of your **mind**, that you may prove what the will of God is, that which is good and acceptable and perfect.
>
> **Ephesians 4:23:** and that you be renewed in the spirit of your **mind**.

To change your mind in the Bible sense of the word is to change your whole inward attitude about everything that is spiritually important. It involves a change of mind about God (Acts 17:29-30; 20:21; Rev. 9:20; 16:9), sin (Luke 17:3-4; Acts 8:22; 2 Cor. 12:21; Rev. 2:21-22), righteousness (Rev. 2:5; 3:3), and yes, God's Son (Acts 2:38) too.

Repentance unto life must not be equated with any outward action. It is rather a change of heart that produces outward action. The key thing, however, is the state of a man's mind and heart and soul. Repentance is neither mental gymnastics nor outward religious rituals. It is a change in that thinking soul that guides and rules the whole man and whole life. No amount of penance is repentance. No amount of truly good deeds is repentance if they do not proceed from a profound, heart-deep change of attitude about God, sin, righteousness, and the Savior.

Do not deceive yourself by thinking that mental gymnastics or intellectual calisthenics about the identity of Jesus is true repentance. Do not deceive yourself into thinking that religious activities done with no heart are repentance. Do not deceive yourself into thinking that good deeds are repentance if they do not proceed from a sorrow for sin that has produced a heart-deep change of mind about it.

Do not deceive yourself—finally—into thinking that good works are the condition of forgiveness and salvation. It is because repentance is fundamentally a change of heart that it is consistent with the idea of salvation by faith alone. Some in our day are using the doctrine of repentance to contradict the idea that we are justified by faith alone. The requirement of repentance by the gospel means, they think, that our good works are a condition of forgiveness. They reason that repentance is a change in our lifestyle embodied in good works. Then they remind their listeners that repentance is the condition of forgiveness (Luke 13:3, 5; 24:47). They conclude that good works are the condition of being forgiven. The flaw in this deviant line of reasoning is the idea that repentance is ***not*** fundamentally a change in our lifestyle consisting in good works. Repentance is a change of mind and heart. It does not essentially consist in good deeds. Forgiveness is bestowed on this change of heart and mind prior to any good works. Thus, the foundational doctrine of salvation by grace through faith without works is maintained and the fallacy of a potentially fatal line of reasoning is exposed.

If you would repent, you must have a deep heart change about God, your sin, righteousness, and Jesus Christ. You must reject with grief your previous attitudes about them and adopt a new respect for God's law, a new sorrow for your sin, a new sense of your own personal need for Jesus Christ. This alone is true repentance.

CHAPTER 9:

ON THE FOLIAGE OF REPENTANCE

The tree of repentance has foliage. By foliage I mean the leaves which show that the tree is alive. These leaves are not to be mistaken for the fruit of a transformed lifestyle which is the true evidence of repentance. Yet, they are the God-appointed adornment of the tree of repentance.

What am I talking about? I am talking about baptism. Leaves or foliage manifest the return of life to trees in northern climates. When the tree of repentance comes to life, the foliage springs out of its branches. That foliage is according to the New Testament, baptism in water. Nine times in the New Testament repentance and baptism are mentioned together within two verses. Five times John's baptism is called a baptism of repentance.

> **Matthew 3:11:** "As for me, I **baptize** you with water for **repentance**, but He who is coming after me is mightier than I, and I am not fit to remove His sandals; He will **baptize** you with the Holy Spirit and fire.

> **Mark 1:4:** John the **Baptist** appeared in the wilderness preaching a **baptism** of **repentance** for the forgiveness of sins.

> **Luke 3:3:** And he came into all the district around the Jordan, preaching a **baptism** of **repentance** for the forgiveness of sins;

> **Acts 13:24:** after John had proclaimed before His coming a **baptism** of **repentance** to all the people of Israel.

> **Acts 19:4:** And Paul said, "John **baptized** with the **baptism** of **repentance**, telling the people to believe in Him who was coming after him, that is, in Jesus."

But it is not just John's baptism that was a baptism of repentance. What is some times distinguished as Christian baptism is also a baptism of repentance.

> **Acts 2:38:** And Peter *said* to them, "**Repent**, and let each of you be **baptized** in the name of Jesus Christ for the forgiveness of your sins; and you shall receive the gift of the Holy Spirit.

Someone once asked me about the fact that baptism is mentioned so frequently in the key passages on repentance. This person wondered aloud if we should not talk about *the three things* that you must do to be saved. I disagreed with the person, and he quickly agreed that we should not make baptism equal in saving importance with faith and repentance.

Let me make clear why I disagreed with saying that baptism is a third thing one must do to be saved. It is true, of course, that in Acts 20:21 baptism is not mentioned. This is significant. More important, however, is the clear fact that we know men can be saved and have been saved without baptism. All the Old Testament saints were saved without being baptized. Even circumcision (which some might think of as a kind of Old Testament baptism) was not necessary to be saved. Abraham was saved without it. Circumcision for Abraham was merely the outward sign that He had been justified (Romans 4:9-11).

> [9] Is this blessing then on the circumcised, or on the uncircumcised also? For we say, "FAITH WAS CREDITED TO ABRAHAM AS RIGHTEOUSNESS." [10] How then was it credited? While he was circumcised, or uncircumcised? Not while circumcised, but while uncircumcised; [11] and he received the sign of circumcision, a seal of the righteousness of the faith which he had while uncircumcised, so that he might be the father of all who believe without being circumcised, that righteousness might be credited to them

Even after Christ came to earth, men were saved without baptism. The thief on the cross was saved without baptism (Luke 23:40-43). Paul did not rank baptism as a matter on a level with the faith and repentance required by the gospel. This is why he could rejoice that he had baptized few or none of the Corinthian believers (1 Corinthians 1:14-17).

> [14] I thank God that I baptized none of you except Crispus and Gai-

> us, [15] so that no one would say you were baptized in my name. [16] Now I did baptize also the household of Stephanas; beyond that, I do not know whether I baptized any other. [17] For Christ did not send me to baptize, but to preach the gospel, not in cleverness of speech, so that the cross of Christ would not be made void.

So baptism is not strictly necessary to salvation. Nevertheless, the person who approached me wondering about the close relationship of baptism and repentance did have a point. In the New Testament baptism is closely associated with repentance. It is the foliage of repentance.

Why is there such a close relationship between repentance and baptism in the New Testament? The simplest answer is that this close relationship is commanded by Jesus Christ. In the Great Commission found in Matthew 28:18-20 He commanded that His disciples must be baptized.

> [18] And Jesus came up and spoke to them, saying, "All authority has been given to Me in heaven and on earth. [19] Go therefore and make disciples of all the nations, baptizing them in the name of the Father and the Son and the Holy Spirit, [20] teaching them to observe all that I commanded you; and lo, I am with you always, even to the end of the age."

This is why His apostles ordered people to be baptized when they repented and believed the gospel. Peter, for instance, ordered that the Gentiles of Cornelius' household should be baptized, after they believed and received the gift of the Spirit in Acts 10:48.

> And he ordered them to be baptized in the name of Jesus Christ. Then they asked him to stay on for a few days.

For the comfort and encouragement of believers and to declare their faith to the world God has been pleased to connect the blessings of His covenants with tangible outward signs. In the New Covenant it is clear that He has connected the blessings of salvation through the New Covenant in Christ with the outward sign of baptism. Knowingly to refuse this sign is to disobey Jesus Christ and reject the comfort and confession of Christ before the world which is embodied in this sign. Thus, while baptism is not strictly speaking one of the two things you must do to be saved, it is a very bad sign when someone knowing what Christ commands refuses to be baptized. It raises serious questions, indeed! Does such a person really love Christ? Are they really saved?

> **John 14:15:** If you love Me, you will keep My commandments.

> **John 14:24:** He who does not love Me does not keep My words; and the word which you hear is not Mine, but the Father's who sent Me.

> **John 15:13-14:** Greater love has no one than this, that one lay down his life for his friends. You are My friends if you do what I command you.

Those men and women who have repented of their sins should make haste to put on the sign of repentance by being baptized in water. One who has repented of his sins, but who is not baptized is like a living tree without its green foliage. Perhaps such a person is alive spiritually, but he looks dead.

I remember when I lived in Michigan that our church was visited by some Philippino friends. They had never seen winter or snow before. It was all very different for them. They had also never seen living trees without leaves before. All the trees looked dead to them as they stood there leafless in the dead of winter. The trees may have been alive, but they looked dead to our Philippino friends because they lacked the foliage they associated with living trees.

If you have truly repented of your sins, but have not been baptized you should with all due haste take care of your inconsistent situation, your *leafless* and dead-looking condition. Honor Christ and show others that you are alive spiritually by being baptized!

CHAPTER 10:

ON THE FRUITS OF REPENTANCE

One of the main reasons that the doctrine of repentance in the Bible suggests the analogy of a tree is the emphasis of the New Testament on the fact that true repentance bears fruit. The tree of repentance is a fruit tree!

This reality is emphasized in the Shorter Catechism mentioned in an earlier chapter. It affirms: *Repentance unto life is a saving grace, whereby a sinner, out of a true sense of his sin, and apprehension of the mercy of God in Christ, doth, with grief and hatred of his sin,* ***turn from it unto God, with full purpose of, and endeavor after, new obedience.*** The words I have placed in bold emphasize the idea that true repentance is a tree that bears the fruit of new obedience to God.

There are two ways at least in which the New Testament makes clear that the tree of repentance is a fruit tree.

The first is by means of the several passages that speak of works fitting for repentance. Notice especially the parts of the verses below which I have placed in bold and italicized.

> **Matthew 3:8:** "Therefore ***bring forth fruit in keeping with repentance***...
>
> **Luke 3:8:** "Therefore ***bring forth fruits in keeping with repentance***, and do not begin to say to yourselves, 'We have Abraham for our father,' for I say to you that God is able from these stones to raise up children to Abraham.
>
> **Acts 26:20:** but *kept* declaring both to those of Damascus first, and *also* at Jerusalem and *then* throughout all the region of Judea, and *even* to the Gentiles, that they should repent and turn to God, ***performing deeds appropriate to repentance***.

Those who are repenting are commanded to bring forth fruit in keeping with repentance. Since this fruit is in keeping with repentance, the lack of it raises the most serious questions about the authenticity of one's repentance.

The second way in which the New Testament makes clear that repentance is a fruit tree is by another word it uses to mean repentance. We have already looked at the word that means remorse or sorrow. We have looked also at the main New Testament word for repentance which means a change of mind and heart. There is a third word used to refer to conversion or repentance. It is the word that means to turn or return. Notice the way in which the main word for repentance is associated with the word meaning to turn or return in the following passages.

> **Acts 26:20:** but *kept* declaring both to those of Damascus first, and *also* at Jerusalem and *then* throughout all the region of Judea, and *even* to the Gentiles, that they should ***repent*** and ***turn*** to God, performing deeds appropriate to repentance.

> **Acts 3:19:** "***Repent*** therefore and ***return***, that your sins may be wiped away, in order that times of refreshing may come from the presence of the Lord;

> **Luke 17:4:** "And if he sins against you seven times a day, and ***returns*** to you seven times, saying, 'I ***repent***,' forgive him."

Thus, repentance is attributed to the Thessalonians in 1 Thessalonians 1:9: "For they themselves report about us what kind of a reception we had with you, and how you turned to God from idols to serve a living and true God."

This word meaning to turn or return makes clear that every true change of mind is followed by a change of will and spiritual direction. To turn is to change your direction. To turn requires an act of will. Repentance involves turning from sin to God. Repentance means that the spiritual direction of your life is altered. You were going toward sin and now you are going toward God. Clearly, this means that the tree of repentance is a fruit tree. This new direction and the works that manifest it are "the fruits in keeping with repentance."

Of course, this new spiritual direction is not perfect, but it is real.

It is like the Mississippi River. What direction does the Mississippi River flow? Everyone knows that basically it flows south into the Gulf of Mexico from where it originates in Minnesota. But if you look at a map, you will see places where it flows east and west and even back north. Yet its basic and overall direction is south. The deviations do not change this fact. It is just so with the one who repents. There is, in spite of all the inconsistencies, a new, basic, overall direction to his life.

This suggests to me a final question. Have you really turned? Has your basic, spiritual direction been altered? Is there a new direction in your life since you say you have become a Christian? This is the great and decisive question about the genuineness of your Christianity. Have you turned to God from idols to serve the living and true God (1 Thess. 1:9)? There is a necessary heart turn in repentance that leads to an inevitable life turn.

> **1 Thessalonians 1:9-10:** For they themselves report about us what kind of a reception we had with you, and how you ***turned*** to God from idols to serve a living and true God, and to wait for His Son from heaven, whom He raised from the dead, *that is* Jesus, who rescues us from the wrath to come.

If you have not, then no longer delay and no longer deceive yourself! Change your mind about God, sin, and Christ. Turn—actually turn—from sin to Christ and to God first in your heart and then in your life!

If we would be faithful evangelists to others, we cannot omit the biblical perspective that repentance is a fruit tree. We cannot fail to tell men that true repentance and a true heart turning to God always results in a new spiritual direction in a person's life. The new spiritual direction of life is not the condition of being saved. It is not the essence of repentance. It is not the *root*. It is, however, the inevitable *fruit* of true repentance.

CHAPTER 11:

ON THE ARROW OF FAITH

Acts 20:21 speaks of both *repentance toward God and faith toward our Lord Jesus Christ.* With this chapter we come in this study to the second of these two things everyone must do to be saved. We come to what Paul calls *faith toward our Lord Jesus Christ.*

In order to make the different features of this second thing we must do to be saved more memorable, let me ask that you think of faith as an arrow. Thinking of the arrow of faith will help you, I hope, remember the five things I want to say about faith.

In this part of our studies we will think, first, of the origin of faith. We will, in other words, ask the question, *Where does faith come from?* Here I want you to think of the quiver from which the arrow of faith is drawn. Like its Siamese twin grace of repentance, we will see that faith is the gift of God's sovereign grace. The quiver of faith is sovereign grace. No man believes except through the mighty drawing grace of God. Just as Jesus Himself said, "No one can come to Me unless the Father who sent Me draws him" (John 6:44).

We will consider, in the second place, the object of faith. I will liken this to the arrowhead. It is the arrowhead which is the crucial aspect of the arrow—without which it cannot accomplish its purpose. It is even so with the object of faith. Acts 20:21 teaches that the object of faith is *the Lord Jesus Christ.* The saving thing about saving faith is not faith, but the object of faith, the Lord Jesus Christ.

In the third place, we will look at the nature of faith. I liken this in my mind to the shaft of the arrow. Though faith is not the main thing, still faith is necessary and has a clear and crucial nature in the Bible. The Bible, however, pictures saving faith in two supplementary or complementary ways. I will argue that true faith involves both conviction of the truth of the gospel and commitment (entrustment) to the Christ of the gospel.

Fourthly, I will speak of the instrumentality of faith. The Bible in all sorts of ways emphasizes that there is something uniquely and even exclusively important about faith. Protestants believe that the Bible teaches justification by faith alone. In this chapter I intend to raise the question of why faith is the unique and exclusive instrument of justification. I will liken this to the feathers which help the arrow fly straight and true to its intended goal.

That intended goal, in the fifth place, will be likened to the target of the arrow of faith. I will argue that God has a reason for creating a way of salvation that is by faith alone. It is that men might come to an assurance of their salvation. God wants not only to save men, but that men might know that they are saved. This is, as I said, the intended target of the arrow of faith.

This discussion of the assurance of salvation that God intends to give through faith requires as a sixth chapter of this part of the book a discussion of the difference between saving faith and false faith. I will attempt in this chapter to make clear the distinguishing differences between the true and counterfeit faith.

CHAPTER 12:

ON THE ORIGIN OF FAITH—THE QUIVER

In our examination of the tree of repentance we saw that the soil of the tree of repentance is the sovereign grace of God. Since repentance and faith are Siamese twins it should not surprise us to learn that they have the same womb or origin. Saving faith is also the gift of God's sovereign grace. When a man's heart is humbled to see his need of Christ and to embrace Christ for salvation in saving faith, this is not due to the fact that he is better, wiser, or more lucky than his fellow sinners. God is to be given credit for such faith. The arrow of faith comes out of the quiver of God's sovereign grace. This is the teaching of Scripture everywhere, but in the mouth of two or three witnesses let every fact be confirmed. Please consider several texts with me.

The first text is Philippians 1:29:

> For to you it has been granted for Christ's sake, not only to believe in Him, but also to suffer for His sake

Here there is the explicit statement of the Apostle Paul that faith is a grant or gift from God. To suffer for Christ is a gift of grace. To be chosen to suffer for Him is a privilege which reaps the great reward of reigning with Him (Rom. 8:17; 2 Tim. 2:12). But just as suffering with Christ is a grant from God's grace, so also is believing in Christ. Such faith is given to men for the sake of what Christ did for them on the cross. In order that Christ should see fruit from His redemptive sufferings God gives men faith. Faith is the gift of God!

John 3:3-5 is the second passage:

> 3 Jesus answered and said to him, "Truly, truly, I say to you, unless one is born again he cannot see the kingdom of God." 4 Nicodemus said to Him, "How can a man be born when he is old? He cannot enter a second time into his mother's womb and be born, can he?" 5 Jesus answered, "Truly, truly, I say to you, unless one is born of water and the Spirit he cannot enter into the kingdom of God."

How does a man enter the kingdom of God? He enters the kingdom by faith. Here Jesus teaches that to enter the kingdom by faith a man must first be born again. How does a man see the kingdom of God? Again, it is clear from Scripture that one sees the kingdom with the eyes of faith. Here Jesus also teaches explicitly that the eyes of faith are bestowed by the new birth.

Something else must be noticed here. The analogy of birth clearly suggests that in the inception or origin of faith the sinner is *not* the actor, *but the one acted upon*. Faith is like the breath of the soul. Of course, the baby must breathe to live. But babies do not give birth to themselves. Even so God is the one that gives the new birth to the sinner and breathes into his nostrils the breath of faith and makes him live and breathe.

You may have been taught that men are born again *by faith*. This clearly suggests that faith logically precedes the new birth. Jesus' teaching suggests just the opposite. Faith itself is the gift of the new birth. We are not born again by faith. We are born again to faith. Even though faith and the new birth cannot be separated in time, faith logically and causally follows the new birth. Vice versa, the new birth is the cause of faith.

At the same time, as I just said, there is no spiritual life apart from faith. Faith and spiritual life are inseparable.

> **John 20:31:** but these have been written so that you may believe that Jesus is the Christ, the Son of God; and ***that believing you may have life in His name***.

Therefore, though we are not born again *by faith*, we are born again *in faith*. That is to say, it is by giving us faith in the Lord Jesus Christ that God the Father gives us the new birth. The new birth cleanses us. That is why Jesus speaks of it as being born of "water and Spirit." Water here (as in the Old Testament passage of which Jesus is thinking) speaks of cleansing.

> **Ezekiel 36:25-27:** Then I will sprinkle clean water on you, and you will be clean; I will cleanse you from all your filthiness and from all your idols. [26] Moreover, I will give you a new heart and put a new spirit within you; and I will remove the heart of stone

> from your flesh and give you a heart of flesh. [27] I will put My Spirit within you and cause you to walk in My statutes, and you will be careful to observe My ordinances.

Thus, we may say that it is through giving us faith in Christ that God cleanses our hearts in the new birth.

> **Acts 15:9:** and He made no distinction between us and them, cleansing their hearts by faith.

Perhaps an illustration may help here. When you were young, you may have, like me, accidentally thrown or knocked a ball through someone's window. The ball caused the window to break, but you cannot separate the breaking of the window from the ball hitting it in time. The ball hit the window, and the window broke, *at the same time*. So also faith and the new birth are inseparable in time, but the new birth logically and causally precedes faith.

The very faith by which we see and enter the kingdom is a gift given by the new birth. Saving faith is drawn out of the quiver of God's sovereign grace.

Please do not misunderstand what I have been saying. Nothing that I have said denies that it is our activity and duty to believe in Christ. Clearly, as I have been saying, believing is one of the two things we must do to be saved. Nor should we wonder, if we want to be saved, about whether God will give us faith. If we wish to be saved (and even if we don't), we are invited to place our faith in Christ. *A true desire to believe is an indication that God is giving us faith.* The only thing that prevents men from believing is their unwillingness to do so. Whosever will may come! The meaning of God giving men faith is that God makes them willing to receive Christ. If you are willing, there is no reason to worry.

The fact that faith is the gift of God means positively that if you do believe, God should receive all the glory for your being a believer. It means that the one who believes is the object of God's special love and grace. If you believe, it means that you are the object of God's special love and grace. You should rejoice in and worship before the God of such love!

John Piper's hymn is true when it says:

All-sovereign grace saved us in Christ,
Before our birth pure grace sufficed,
Not from our deeds that man enthralls
Or from our faith, but him who calls.

The old gospel song also says this very well:

I know not how the Spirit moves,
Convincing men of sin,
Revealing Jesus through His Word,
Creating faith in him

But I know whom I have believed
And am persuaded that He is able
To keep that which I've committed
Unto him against that day

CHAPTER 13:

ON THE OBJECT OF FAITH—THE ARROWHEAD

One of the most striking things in Acts 20:21 is the contrast between the object of repentance and the object of faith. This contrast is especially clear in the Greek, because the same preposition is used to describe first the object or focus of repentance and then the object or focus of faith. The Greek may be literally translated, "repentance **toward** God and faith **toward** our Lord Jesus Christ." Repentance is directed toward God. Faith is directed toward our Lord Jesus Christ. Please do not misunderstand me. There is no absolute contrast. Repentance could also be said to be directed toward the Lord Jesus Christ. Faith could also be said to be directed toward God. But there is a reason by way of propriety why Paul puts it the way he does.

Repentance has for its focus God. Sin is against God, the law-giver. He it is that is displeased and offended with sin and who is determined to punish it. Thus, it is toward God that repentance is directed. Had Jesus never become incarnate to be our Savior, there would still have been sin and the duty to repent of it.

Faith has for its object the Lord Jesus. The focus of saving faith is on the Savior of men. Thus, faith toward the Lord Jesus is not faith in God in the abstract. It is not faith in God as law-giver. Nor is it even faith in God as Creator. All this may be said to be assumed in faith, but the saving faith of which Paul is speaking is faith in the God who was in Christ reconciling the world to Himself.

> **2 Corinthians 5:18-21:** Now all *these* things are from God, who reconciled us to Himself through Christ and gave us the ministry of reconciliation, [19] namely, that God was in Christ reconciling the world to Himself, not counting their trespasses against them, and He has committed to us the word of reconciliation. [20] Therefore, we are ambassadors for Christ, as though God were making an appeal through us; we beg you on behalf of Christ, be reconciled to God. [21] He made Him who knew no sin *to be* sin on our behalf, so that we might become the righteousness of God in Him.

Thus, the focus of faith is the Lord Jesus. In this name is summed up all He is as the Redeemer. He is the Lord. He is the one who is God with power and authority to save. He is Jesus. This is His human name given Him at birth. As Matthew 1:21 says, "You shall call His name Jesus, because He shall save His people from their sins." He is man so that he can be our substitutionary sin-bearer. He is the one man set apart by God to be our prophet, priest, and king. He is our prophet to instruct our ignorance. He is our priest to be both substitutionary sacrifice on earth and interceding high priest for them in heaven. He is our king to deliver us from our enemies beginning with the enemy of sin.

Any discussion of faith must begin with a discussion of its object. Faith is an empty cup, an empty circle, and an empty hand. It signifies nothing and does nothing apart from Christ. Let me say it again. The virtue or attitude of faith is nothing. Faith in itself and by itself does not save. Faith in Christ saves. We may even say Christ saves us through faith. Faith is an eye in a universe where there is nothing to see without the Lord Jesus Christ.

It is true that in some places the Bible seems to speak of faith as saving us. Do these passages contradict what I am saying? For instance, Paul seems to say something like this in Romans 4:5.

> **Romans 4:5:** But to the one who does not work, but believes in Him who justifies the ungodly, his faith is credited as righteousness,

Luther's explanation, however, is correct and very true to the teaching of Scripture about faith.

> Faith taketh hold of Christ, and hath him present, and holdeth him inclosed, as the ring doth the precious stone. And whosoever shall be found having this confidence in Christ apprehended in the heart, him will God account for righteous.

When the Bible speaks of faith, it is speaking of faith as a ring that has set in it the precious stone of Jesus Christ. Thus, the Bible may speak only of the ring (faith), but the ring (faith) always includes the stone (Jesus Christ) whether it is mentioned or not. Thus, faith is credited as righteousness because encloses Jesus Christ and His righteousness—not because faith is a sufficient righteousness in itself. Think of it this way. Someone may say, "This ring is worth ten thousand dollars." The ring of which the person is speaking may have a gold band which could be purchased anywhere for one hundred dollars, but in the ring is set a diamond worth around ten thousand dollars. We do not call the person a liar because the band is only one hundred dollars. Everyone realizes that the ring includes the diamond. Even so the Bible can truly say that faith is credited as righteousness, because everyone who knows anything about the Bible knows that faith includes Jesus Christ.

The worst thing that I could do in instructing you about faith is to leave you focusing just on faith itself. The whole point of faith is to focus on Christ. When your vision and mind is filled with Him, when you take Him, come to Him, and run to Him as your Savior, then you have faith.

CHAPTER 14:

ON THE NATURE OF FAITH—THE ARROW SHAFT

Have you ever thought that often there is more than one right way to look at something? Take your car for instance. Take a picture of it as it sits there right now in the parking lot and that picture will be quite different from the one the oil change mechanic could take in his oil pit down at the local instant oil change place. (Don't ask me how weird an oil change mechanic would have to be to do that!) Which picture of your car would be correct? Even though the pictures would be drastically different in most every way, both pictures would be correct. There is more than one way to look at an automobile.

I hope in this chapter to show you that there is more than one correct way to look at saving faith. That is, I want to argue that the Bible gives us two pictures or descriptions of faith. They do not contradict each other, but they complement and supplement each other. Just like those two pictures of your car would give a more complete view of your automobile, so these two biblical descriptions of faith give a more complete view of saving faith. You may think of it this way to build on my arrow illustration: The wood in the arrow shaft of faith has two distinct colors.

Since the Scripture views faith from two complementary or supplementary perspectives, my discussion of saving faith is structured around this dual perspective of Scripture. Here are those dual perspectives.

> *Faith, in the first place, is conviction of the truth of the gospel.*
> *Faith, on the other hand, is commitment to the Christ of the gospel.*

Faith, in the first place, is conviction of the truth of the gospel.

Saving faith is the conviction that the gospel is true. Saving faith, that is to say, fully credits the factuality of the message proclaimed by the preachers of the gospel.

This may be seen clearly in the Old Testament word for faith. The root, *AMAN*, is translated by "faith" or "believe" many times. It fundamentally means to regard something as true or reliable. This is the root used in two occurrences of faith most quoted in the New Testament (Genesis 15:6; Habakkuk 2:4).

> **Genesis 15:6:** Then he believed in the LORD; and He reckoned it to him as righteousness.

> **Habakkuk 2:4:** "Behold, as for the proud one, His soul is not right within him; But the righteous will live by his faith.

It is brought out in the hundreds of places where saving faith is described as "believing that." Saving faith involves "believing that" (Heb. 11:6). It is knowing that something is true. (John 6:69; 10:38; 12:46; 1 John 4:16). It is having your eyes opened to reality (John 12:38, 39).

This is the burden of the classic biblical definition of saving faith:

> **Hebrews 11:1:** Now faith is the assurance of *things* hoped for, the conviction of things not seen.

The two key descriptions of faith in this text (*assurance* and *conviction*) clearly define faith as conviction. The first word which describes faith in this text is properly translated by the NASB as *assurance*. It is very similar in its meaning to the Old Testament word for faith noted above, *AMAN*. Greek lexicons give the meanings "confidence, conviction, assurance, or steadfastness" for this word. The second word used in this text is properly translated as *conviction*. Greek lexicons provide the translations "proof or conviction" (Jude 15; Titus 1:9).

Some have thought that the Bible uses "believe" to designate a false faith, while "believe in" is used to designate a true faith. Not so! Saving faith may be described as believing that *Jesus is the Son of God* (1 John 5:5). One proper way to look at faith is to see it as a conviction of the truth of the gospel.

Faith, on the other hand, is commitment to the Christ of the gospel.

Faith is not only or simply or merely believing that the gospel is true. It is not just conviction of the truth of the gospel. It is also commitment to the Christ of the gospel. Commitment here means the act of entrusting ourselves to Christ. John Murray's excellent remarks crystallize the matter.

> Faith must rise to trust, and to trust that consists in entrustment to him. In faith there is the engagement of person to person in the inner movement of the whole man to receive and rest upon Christ alone for salvation. It means the abandonment of confidence in our own or any human resources in a totality act of self-commitment to Christ.

Faith is the believing abandonment of ourselves to Christ in a way that may seem a terrible risk to because we have never trusted anyone but ourselves! Faith is, then, abandoning ourselves to Christ in spite of every risk and as the salvation from every danger. Faith is the believing abandonment of every other hope but Christ and the consigning of our whole destiny into the hand of Jesus Christ. It is taking the parachute of Christ and jumping out of the burning airplane of our sinful lives.

Four considerations indicate that faith means commitment:

(1) The use of the Greek word which is usually translated, believe, to mean entrust or commit indicates that believing involves an act of commitment. Note, for instance, the play on words found in John 2:23-25.

> [23] Now when He was in Jerusalem at the Passover, during the feast, many believed in His name, observing His signs which He was doing. [24] But Jesus, on His part, was not entrusting Himself to them, for He knew all men, [25] and because He did not need anyone to testify concerning man, for He Himself knew what was in man.

What is the play on words in verses 23 and 24? Crucial to understanding it is realizing that the word translated by the NASB *believed* in verse 23 is the same word as that translated *entrusting* in verse 24. The meaning of this play on words may be brought out in the sentence: *They believed in Christ, but He did not believe in them.* Since the word for believe is properly translated *entrust*, it is clear that the idea of entrusting yourself to someone is contained in the idea of believing in someone.

2 Timothy 1:12 also associates entrusting with believing. Though the word translated *entrusted* there is not the same as the word translated *entrusted* in John 2:24, the close association of believing with the idea of entrustment is also clearly brought out in 2 Tim.1:12. In that text "believed and entrusted" are used as synonyms. Notice this from their being placed in bold in the following citation.

> 12 For this reason I also suffer these things, but I am not ashamed; for I know whom I have **believed** and I am convinced that He is able to guard what I have **entrusted** to Him until that day.

(2) The frequent occurrence of the phrase, *believe into*, conveys the idea of commitment (John 2:11; 3:16, 18, 36; 4:39; 6:29). This phrase is often translated into English as *believe in*. But in Greek this phrase may be more literally translated *believe into*. The Greek preposition *eis* often conveys the idea of movement *into* something. Thus, this Greek phrase (*believe into*) clearly conveys the idea of a spiritual movement toward the object of faith. Murray remarks that this phrase "bears the notion of 'movement towards'." Warfield says, "In any event, what these passages express is an "absolute transference of trust from ourselves to another, a complete self surrender to Christ."

(3) The frequent occurrence of the phrase, *believe upon*, (Luke 24:25; Rom. 4:5) conveys the idea of reliance and, thus, of the entrusting commitment which resting upon Christ implies. Here the Greek preposition is *epi* which is usually translated upon. Used in conjunction with the verb for believe it conveys the idea of resting and reliance.

Jesus contrasts the disturbance of soul experienced by the doubting disciples on the road to a village named Emmaus in Luke 24:13 with "believing upon" the prophets in Luke 24:25. Their disturbance and restlessness of soul is the opposite of the calm reliance that such faith would have given them.

(4) The analogies or illustrations used in parallel with believing show that it is more than a mere persuasion of truth. It clearly also includes and involves an act of the will and a movement of the soul. In John 1:12 believing is parallel with *receiving* Christ and contrasted with rejecting His claims. (Cf. v. 11) In John 6:35, 64, and 65 believing is *coming* to Christ, availing ourselves of the provision made for us and our salvation by him. In John 6:47-51, 53 believing is *eating* the Bread of Life and *drinking* His blood. Thus, it is a personal appropriation of the provision made by Christ for our spiritual needs. The common element in each of these analogies is that believing involves a movement of the will. It is reception, coming, and appropriation.

Faith, then, is a conviction which moves us to an appropriate response. It is not the merely passive persuasion of our intellects. It is not mere assent to certain doctrines. It is a whole-souled conviction of the truth leading to a heart commitment to the Christ of the gospel.

What is the relation of these two descriptions of faith?

If faith is commitment to Christ (and nothing less than that), how can the Bible sometimes describe saving faith as a conviction of the truth? On the other hand, if faith is conviction, why does the Bible sometimes describe it as a commitment made by the will to Christ? The Bible can describe saving faith as either conviction or commitment because the one always carries with it the other.

Saving faith is sometimes viewed as a simple conviction of the truth because the Bible assumes that if we are really convinced of the truth of something, we will respond appropriately. It assumes that all true conviction involves commitment. The conviction that the building we are in is on fire will lead, if it is genuine, to the commitment to escape it.

Saving faith is sometimes viewed as commitment because there are people who say that they are convinced of certain things but do not act appropriately. They need to know that faith involves commitment. The kind of conviction that does not lead you to use the fire escape from a burning building is not true conviction. The kind of faith that does not cause you to come to Christ is not saving faith.

What do we learn from this?

(1) The biblical emphasis on saving faith as "believing that" is a healthy antidote to the tendency of some to make faith a very subjective and mystical matter. Saving faith is the conviction that the gospel is true. Is the gospel reality to you? Do you live as if it were true? Then you have faith. It is nothing more complicated than that.

(2) On the other hand, the biblical emphasis on saving faith as "believing in, into, or upon" guards against the tendency of others to reduce faith to mere mental assent to biblical propositions. Faith is not a sterile, emotionless, passive, and stationary kind of thing. It is a knowing that moves you. It takes you into Christ.

(3) Conviction is the test of commitment. There are many in our day who are supposedly "committed Christians," who do not believe in the great truths of Christianity: creation, sin, hell, or the deity, atonement, or resurrection of Christ. The commitment of such people is phony and cannot lead to a valid, lasting, and true walk in the way of Christ.

(4) Commitment is the test of conviction. If you say that you believe the Bible, your life will be radically altered by its truths. Your faith as conviction of the truth of the gospel will lead to a whole-souled commitment to Christ as Savior and Lord. If it does not, your faith is phony.

(5) Truth is central in saving faith. Faith is regarding something as true. You cannot believe what you are not aware of. You cannot remain committed to that of which you are not convinced. We must know the truths of God's Word if we are to have faith. We must teach the truths of God's Word if we are to help others believe.

(6) Faith involves an act of the will. Well-known (and purportedly Reformed) writers have taught that faith is a passive persuasion of the mind and that it is legalism to view faith as an act of the will. Clearly, however, the Bible teaches that faith is a movement of the will toward Christ, as well as a perception of the mind about Christ. Faith involves a personal appropriation of Christ. It is not enough to smell, admire, or talk about the gospel meal. We must eat it, otherwise it will not save us. Faith also involves a personal relationship with Christ. It is entrusting ourselves to another person. It is entrusting yourself to Christ's protection and leadership.

Conclusion:

Do you have saving faith? Have you personally become convinced in your heart of the truth of the gospel? Have you personally entrusted yourself to Jesus Christ as savior and Lord? Have you personally appropriated Christ for your needs?

Let me put it this way. Have you eaten the gospel meal? It is not enough it to smell it, talk about it, admire it, or compliment the chef. Unless you actually take up the spoon of faith and eat the gospel meal, it will not save you. Have you actually eaten the gospel meal?

These are the great questions with which this chapter confronts us. They are also the great questions with which every evangelist must confront those he would win to Christ and salvation.

CHAPTER 15:

ON THE INSTRUMENTALITY OF FAITH—THE ARROW FEATHERS

The single great issue that broke the church in two at the time of the Reformation was the issue of justification by faith alone. In the climactic confessions of faith flowing out of the Reformation (the Westminster Confession and its daughter confessions the Savoy Declaration and the 1689 Baptist Confession) the issue of justification by faith alone was stated this way at chapter 11, paragraph 2: "Faith ... is the alone instrument of justification; yet it is not alone in the person justified, but is ever accompanied with all other saving graces."

In this chapter we come to the instrumentality of faith. When we use this big word *instrumentality*, we are talking about the fact that we are justified by faith alone. Before I come to open up a key text on this subject let me mention four things by way of introduction to this subject.

The Meaning of Instrumentality

The word, *instrumentality*, sounds big and technical. Actually, the idea it conveys is very simple. *Instrumentality* speaks of faith as the vehicle, means, or medium by which we come into possession of Christ and God's salvation. All God's salvation is in Christ. We must have Christ to have God's salvation. The salvation is not in our faith. That is only the instrument. The salvation is in Christ. Faith is merely the way or means by which we come into possession of Christ.

Let me illustrate this from something in my own experience. Several years ago I was ministering in the Caribbean nation of Trinidad and Tobago. After I had preached and lectured about 20 times in six days, the brethren there wishing to give me a day of rest took me to the wonderful island of Tobago. There for the first time I went snorkeling. Though I swallowed what seemed like half the Caribbean Sea before I learned to use the snorkel properly, it was in the end a delightful experience. Snorkeling confirmed for me the great truth that in order to see the fish that inhabit the sea you had to have your head under water and be able to breathe at the same time. The snorkel enables you to breathe air while you are under water. It is the instrument by which oxygen is transmitted to your lungs. You do not breathe the snorkel. You breathe through the snorkel. The key thing is the air. The snorkel is merely the instrumental means of your being able to breathe under water.

Faith is similar. What you need to be justified is Christ. Faith is merely the means or the instrumental cause by which you are able to have Christ and His righteousness. It is Christ and His righteousness that is the key thing. It is Christ and His righteousness which saves us. It is faith and faith alone which is the instrumental means by which Christ becomes ours. The instrumentality of faith is a way of saying that faith is the secondary cause and subordinate means of salvation in Christ.

The Preeminence of Faith for Protestant Christians

In this book I have spoken clearly and deliberately about the two things you must do to be saved. In order to be saved one must both repent and believe the gospel. Nevertheless, Protestant Christians have recognized that the Bible places a special emphasis on the place of faith in salvation. Christians do not normally speak of saving repentance, but of saving faith. They do not speak of being justified by repentance alone, but of being justified by faith alone. Both repentance and faith are necessary, but it is somehow faith that has the place of prominence in the way Christians think about these things. In some unique sense, we may assert that faith is *the instrumental means* of salvation. This is why Luther and the Reformation maintained that "faith ... is the alone instrument of justification."

The Prominence of Faith in the Bible

The Bible abundantly confirms the assertion that faith in Christ is the instrumental means of salvation. This is indicated by the fact that the faith root occurs well over 600 times in the New Testament. It is clear from the New Testament that faith holds a strategic and central place in the economy of salvation. We are saved by faith (Rom. 1:16, 17; 10:9; Eph. 2:8). We will be saved by faith (1 Pet. 1:8, 9; Heb. 10:38, 39). We received eternal life by faith (John 20:31). We live by faith (Gal. 2:20; 3:11). All the components of this salvation or eternal life are ours by faith: justification (Rom. 3:28; 4:5; 5:1), forgiveness (Acts 10:43; 26:18), adoption (Gal. 3:26; Rom. 8:14-16) reception of the Spirit, (Gal. 3:2, 5, 14, 22; Eph. 1:13; John 7:39), and perseverance (Heb. 4:3; 6:12; 10:39; 1 Pet. 1:5). Clearly, saving faith occupies a central and strategic place in the economy of salvation.

The Uniqueness of Faith

Why, however, is faith the instrumental means of salvation? Why do we speak and sing of being justified by faith alone?

> Fountain of never-ceasing grace. Thy saints' exhaustless theme
> Great object of immortal praise essentially supreme
> We bless Thee for the glorious fruits Thy incarnation gives
> The righteousness which grace imputes and faith alone receives

Or

> To Jesus we for refuge flee
> Who from the curse has set us free
> And humbly worship at his throne
> Saved by His grace through faith alone

Why faith alone? That is the question. And Romans 4:16 is the pointed, biblical response to this question. The key words in this verse are italicized: "*For this reason it is by faith, in order that it may be in accordance with grace*, so that the promise will be guaranteed to all the descendants, not only to those who are of the Law, but also to those who are of the faith of Abraham, who is the father of us all." In this chapter I want you to notice five things about this important text.

The Question Answered by the Text

The text clearly is intended to answer the very question we have just raised. The Greek may be translated *on account of this it is out of faith*. The NASB translates *for this reason it is by faith*. The ESV translates *that is why it is by faith*. All of these translations assume the question, *Why is justification by faith?* To put this question more contextually, *Why was Abraham, why is all his spiritual seed, justified by faith and not something else?*

The Answer Not Given by the Text

When I speak of the answer not given by the text, I mean that there is an answer to the question, *Why faith?* which some might expect it to give, but which is not the one given by the text. In other words, what I am asking here is, "What does the text not say or teach?" It does not teach that the reason we are justified by faith is that faith is the gift of God.

Now, of course, faith *is* the gift of God. We have shown that both repentance and faith are the gifts of God's sovereign grace. Yet we are not justified by faith simply because it is the gift of God. Why? Because love, repentance, hope, obedience, and every other Christian grace are also the gifts of God.

For instance, at least three times the New Testament affirms that repentance is the gift of God (Acts 5:31; 11:18; 2 Tim. 2:25). Yet, we are not justified by repentance. Love also is the gift of God's grace. It is shed abroad in our hearts by the Holy Spirit (Rom. 5:5). Yet we are not justified by love. Even though all the other graces like repentance, love, and the fear of God are all gifts of God, they are not the alone instrument of justification. Thus, the fact that it is the gift of God this cannot be the distinctive reason why faith is singled out as the instrumental cause of salvation and justification. Though faith itself is the gift of God (Phil. 1:29), this is not the only or main reason why it is the alone instrument of justification.

The Instruction Supplied by the Text

What, then, does the text say positively? Faith occupies this strategic place of instrumentality in the economy of salvation because it underscores and points to the fact that salvation is by free and sovereign grace. Romans 4:16 is really clear: "in order that it may be in accordance with grace."

In this passage there is an emphatic contrast between law and grace. According to verses 13-15, the preceding context, salvation is not and cannot be through the law. The law does not have the resources to save. The law can damn and destroy. It cannot justify and save. On the other hand, the way of salvation is by grace in contrast to law. Salvation is not by works and law. It is by faith and grace.

Faith is given this central, strategic, exclusive role in justification and salvation because God wants salvation to be (and to be known to be) by grace. Faith is the condition or instrumental cause for this reason. The nature of faith minimizes the danger that the condition which God is pleased to require of men to be saved and justified might detract from or obscure the glory of God's grace.

Salvation has for its great goal the glory of God in His grace. Everything is calculated to achieve the single, great end of the glory of God and the humbling of man in the economy of salvation. This is an important emphasis of Paul in 1 Corinthians 1:29-31. God has so constructed the way of salvation ...

> 29 so that no man may boast before God. 30 But by His doing you are in Christ Jesus, who became to us wisdom from God, and righteousness and sanctification, and redemption, 31 so that, just as it is written, "LET HIM WHO BOASTS, BOAST IN THE LORD."

Similarly, in 2 Corinthians 5:17-21 in an extended description of the way of salvation Paul pointedly remarks in verse 18: "Now all *these* things are from God."

Because salvation is calculated or designed to achieve this goal, it is by faith (Rom. 4:16 with 4:2, 5, 20, 21). Faith makes clear the gracious character of salvation. Its essence is to humbly entrust ourselves to another. One Puritan has called faith a "self-emptying grace" and described it as "a grace that takes a man off himself, and gives all the honor to Christ and free grace." Another has used the word, "extraspective," to describe faith. As I understand this description it is intended to indicate that faith looks outside of itself to another. An introspective person is preoccupied with himself. Someone has graphically said that the introspective person is always looking at his own belly-button! But extraspective faith is not preoccupied with itself, but with Christ.

Faith, then, is the instrumental means of justification because it is nothing in itself. It is only the empty hand that takes Christ. To say it differently, it is only the empty dish that holds the gospel meal. If repentance, love, good works, obedience were made the means of receiving God's salvation, it might appear that these virtues merit salvation. Such virtues inevitably tend to focus attention on themselves. Repentance is so pitiable. Love is so admirable. The fear of God is so pious and religious. Faith, however, focuses all the attention on Christ and grace.

Charles Haddon Spurgeon in his little book, *All of Grace*, wisely says:

> Faith, again, is doubtless selected because it gives all the glory to God. It is of faith that it might be by grace, and it is of grace that there might be no boasting; for God cannot endure pride. "The proud he knoweth afar off," and He has no wish to come nearer to them. He will not give salvation in a way which will suggest or foster pride. Paul saith, "Not of works, lest any man should boast." Now, faith excludes all boasting. The hand which receives charity does not say, "I am to be thanked for accepting the gift"; that would be absurd. When the hand conveys bread to the mouth it does not say to the body, "Thank me; for I feed you." It is a very simple thing that the hand does though a very necessary thing; and it never arrogates glory to itself for what it does. So God has selected faith to receive the unspeakable gift of His grace, because it cannot take to itself any credit, but must adore the gracious God who is the giver of all good. Faith sets the crown upon the right head, and therefore the Lord Jesus was wont to put the crown upon the head of faith, saying, "Thy faith hath saved thee; go in peace."

The Illustration Suggested by the Text

According to the old writers, the best illustrations are biblical illustrations. How can the truth of Romans 4:16 be best biblically illustrated? Let me remind you of Gideon and his army.

Faith is appointed to be the instrumental means of salvation for the same reason that Gideon's army was reduced to three hundred men. Faith, in other words, is like Gideon's three hundred. Why did God tell Gideon to send away the twenty two thousand and then later also the ten thousand? You may know that the text says the twenty two thousand were sent away because they were fearful. You may say that that the ten thousand were sent away because they drank the wrong way. You would be right, but I think you would also miss the main point of the passage. In fact, these reasons were secondary and taken by themselves even a little silly.

The main reason for the divine procedure in minimizing the size of Gideon's army is clearly stated in Judges 7:2 which reads: "And the Lord said to Gideon, `the people who are with you are too many for Me to give Midian into their hands, lest Israel become boastful, saying, My own power has delivered me.'" Similarly, it is the very insignificance of faith in itself that is the reason it is chosen. No one who understands what faith is could think that faith merits or that believers deserve any of the credit for salvation.

The Important Applications of the Text

Here, then, is the rationale for the central, strategic, and in some ways exclusive role of faith in salvation. The meaning of faith alone is that salvation is all of grace. Faith is not something we contribute to a salvation that is mostly grace. Salvation is all of grace. Faith is the gift of ***God's grace*** given to be the instrumental means of receiving ***God's grace*** so that salvation ***by God's grace*** alone might shine out in all its undisguised glory. Faith comes from grace, looks to grace, and places the spotlight on grace. Faith simply receives and rests on grace and, thus, glorifies grace. Justifying faith is not only receptive and recumbent, it is also reflective and extraspective.

Nothing could more clearly emphasize the true reason that faith alone is justifying. It is the exclusive, instrumental cause of justification because it is the grace least likely to obscure the fact that salvation is all of grace. It is the grace that simply reflects grace. Faith is simply the true reflection of grace in the human heart. In this sense it is passive and brings nothing to salvation—merely receiving and resting on it.

There are those today and in the past who say they believe in grace alone and even sovereign grace, but who turn faith into a kind of God-given work or virtue which is the condition of salvation—and that God rewards with salvation. Such a teaching is seriously and perhaps fatally in error. It turns faith into the virtuous condition of salvation and tends to obscure the gracious character of salvation. At the end of the day it turns the gospel of grace into a gospel of the works of virtuous faith.

Do you know anything of the faith that does not work, but believes upon the one who justifies the ungodly? If you do not, I call you now to come and lay your burden down on the one who alone and by Himself can save and justify you, the Lord Jesus Christ.

CHAPTER 16:

ON THE ASSURANCE OF FAITH—THE TARGET

It is the glory of the gospel of Christ that it offers true assurance of salvation to sinners. Calvin said that with regard to salvation two guiding principles must control our understanding. We looked at one of them in the previous chapter. The glory of God's grace, or in other words the honor of Christ, must be maintained in our understanding of salvation. The other of these two guiding principles is taken up in this chapter: the assurance of salvation for the sinner. Here are Calvin's own words:

> "And here two things demand our consideration, that the honor which belongs to Christ should be preserved to him entire and undiminished and that consciences assured of the pardon of their sins, should have peace with God."

Only the doctrine of justification by faith alone satisfies the two criteria for a true doctrine of salvation. Only justification by faith alone gives the entire honor for salvation to Christ. Only this doctrine enables sinners to have assurance of salvation and peace of conscience.

This is why I have likened saving faith to an arrow shot at a target. The target which God intends to hit with the arrow of justification by faith alone is the target of assurance of salvation for the sinner.

It may help you to think of this target as having five concentric rings. In this and the next chapter I will attempt to help you understand the issue of assurance of salvation by making and supporting five assertions about the assurance of faith and the assurance of salvation.

There is a kind of assurance that is the essence of faith, but it is not the assurance of salvation.

Here I want to clear up some confusion about terminology. Some people think that if a person has faith they must also have a prevailing assurance of salvation. They assume that faith essentially involves assurance of salvation. Now if this were true, what would it mean? It would mean that if anyone truly lacked assurance of salvation, they would lack faith. If they lacked faith, they would not be a Christian.

What shall we say to this? The first thing I have to say is to admit that *there is a kind of assurance* that is essential to saving faith. Hebrews 11:1 clearly affirms: "Now faith is the assurance of *things* hoped for, the conviction of things not seen."

So my first response to such people must be to admit that there is a kind of assurance that is certainly of the essence of faith or, in other words, essential to faith. (I will show, however, later in this chapter that this assurance is not the same as assurance of salvation.) You remember that in an earlier chapter we spent a great of time establishing that there are two, supplementary, biblical definitions of faith. What is faith in the Bible? I said that faith in the Bible is defined in two supplementary ways:

> *Faith, in the first place, is conviction of the truth of the gospel.*
> *Faith, on the other hand, is commitment to the Christ of the gospel.*

Consider the assurance of faith in light of these two definitions of faith.

Faith, in the first place, is conviction of the truth of the gospel.

True faith, in other words, does not consist in doubts, but in certainties.

> **Romans 10:9:** that if you confess with your mouth Jesus *as* Lord, and believe in your heart that God raised Him from the dead, you shall be saved; 10 for with the heart man believes, resulting in righteousness, and with the mouth he confesses, resulting in salvation.

> James 1:6: But let him ask in faith without any doubting, for the one who doubts is like the surf of the sea driven and tossed by the wind.

The certainty in which faith consists is certainty or assurance or conviction that the gospel is true. You can't be double-minded about that and have faith. The man who is not sure—who does not have some assurance that—that the great doctrines of the gospel are true is not a Christian. There must be a conviction of heart that is the ruling conviction of the man's life.

What is final authority for you? What are you convinced is the truth? Does the authority of the gospel settle it for you? Answer that question honestly, and you will know if you have true faith.

Faith, on the other hand, is commitment to the Christ of the gospel.

Remember that the other biblical definition of faith is commitment to the Christ of the gospel. There is a kind of assurance in this commitment to Christ. This assurance is not, however, the assurance that I am a Christian already. It is not, in other words, assurance of salvation. Actually, when a man is first going to Christ, he may not have that assurance at all. He may, in fact, be convinced that he is not a Christian. Nevertheless, in commitment to Christ there is a kind of assurance. What kind of assurance is it? True commitment to Christ is certain (has the assurance) that, if I go to Christ, I will be saved. Trusting in the truth of Christ's promise to save, if I believe, is necessary. Thus, when a person goes to Christ, it must be with the confidence that he will be received. You must in other words believe John 6:37:

> All that the Father gives Me shall come to Me, and the one who comes to Me I will certainly not cast out.

Dear friend, you must go to Christ, you may go to Christ, believing and being assured that if you go you will be received.

Now before I leave this first assertion, there is a word of caution and encouragement. This assurance that the gospel is true, and this assurance that Christ receives me when I come to Him, is an assurance that may be assaulted by many doubts. It is an assurance that must struggle against many doubts and fears.

You may ask, "How can a person have assurance and yet have doubts at the same time?" This is similar to another question, "How can a person be a believer and yet struggle with unbelief?" Yet, every believer struggles with unbelief. There is a believer and unbeliever in every Christian's soul. The true believer struggles against his unbelief and condemns it. Mark 9:24 says: "Immediately the boy's father cried out and said, 'I do believe; help my unbelief.'"

Practically, this means several things. Do not condemn yourself if you struggle with doubt, unbelief, and fear! Renounce it. Repent of it. Pray against it! But do not count yourself an unbeliever just because of it. The true believer says, *I believe, help my unbelief.* Do not condemn yourself to hell for having to pray, *help my unbelief,* if you can also say, *I believe.*

There is a kind of assurance, then, which is of the essence of saving faith, but this brings me to my second assertion.

Assurance of salvation is, however, not of the essence of saving faith.

What do we mean by assurance of salvation? Assurance of salvation is knowing or believing that one has eternal life and will enter eternal life at the last day. This knowing that I am saved and will be saved is what John refers to in the following passages.

> **1 John 2:3:** By this we know that we have come to know Him, if we keep His commandments.
>
> **1 John 3:2:** Beloved, now we are children of God, and it has not appeared as yet what we will be. We know that when He appears, we will be like Him, because we will see Him just as He is.
>
> **1 John 3:14:** We know that we have passed out of death into life, because we love the brethren.

If assurance of salvation is knowing one has eternal life, and this is what we mean by assurance, then we must assert that *assurance in the sense of assurance of salvation is not of the essence of saving faith*. Let me give you several arguments that clearly prove this.

The biblical terminology for faith clearly distinguishes faith from assurance of salvation.

There are biblical words that include the idea of personal assurance of assurance. Those words are trust and hope. Notice how the following passages include in trust and hope a personal assurance of salvation.

> **Psalm 31:14:** But as for me, I trust in You, O LORD, I say, "You are my God."

> **Psalm 33:20:** Our soul waits for the LORD; He is our help and our shield. [21] For our heart rejoices in Him, Because we trust in His holy name. [22] Let Your lovingkindness, O LORD, be upon us, According as we have hoped in You.

> **Psalm 52:8:** But as for me, I am like a green olive tree in the house of God; I trust in the lovingkindness of God forever and ever.

> **Psalm 56:3:** When I am afraid, I will put my trust in You. 4 In God, whose word I praise, In God I have put my trust; I shall not be afraid. What can *mere* man do to me?

> **Psalm 56:11:** In God I have put my trust, I shall not be afraid. What can man do to me?

> **Psalm 91:2:** I will say to the LORD, "My refuge and my fortress, My God, in whom I trust!"

> **Psalm 125:1-3:** Those who trust in the LORD Are as Mount Zion, which cannot be moved but abides forever. [2] As the mountains surround Jerusalem, So the LORD surrounds His people From this time forth and forever. [3] For the scepter of wickedness shall not rest upon the land of the righteous, So that the righteous will not put forth their hands to do wrong.

The Bible does not use the words, hope and trust, as the main or central words to refer to saving faith. Faith on the one hand and hope and trust on the other are distinct word families. These words are not interchangeable. These word families are distinct in both the Hebrew and the Greek languages.

The biblical basis of faith is always and only the Word of God.

True faith is faith in the Word of God alone. This clearly shows that faith is not assurance of salvation. Why? Because the Scriptures never, anywhere, assert, for instance, that Sam Waldron possesses eternal life. If they did, then it would be an act of faith for me to believe that and believing that to have assurance. But since the Scriptures never assert that anyone of us by name is a Christian, faith is not assurance of salvation. On this point Donald Macleod remarks:

> It is the same with our assurance of our own sonship. The Bible does not contain an explicit statement to the effect that any of us is a child of God. It says only, "As many as received Christ, to them He gave authority to become children of God." The question on which we require assurance from the Holy Spirit is, do we belong to this group? "God's promises and oaths," wrote Jonathan Edwards, "let them be as sure as they will, cannot give strong hope and comfort to any particular person any further than he can know that those promises are made to him."

Saving faith and assurance have distinctively different definitions and, thus, cannot be the same thing.

Faith is conviction of the truth of the gospel and commitment to the Christ of the gospel. This is clearly not the definition of assurance of salvation. Assurance of salvation is knowing that one is himself saved. Since their definitions are clearly different, assurance of salvation cannot be essential to saving faith.

Assurance of salvation is knowing that one has been saved, but faith is the instrumental means of salvation.

To say that faith involves assurance of salvation is to say that one must believe that one is saved in order to be saved. This is a logical contradiction. A sinner first goes to Christ not because he believes he is saved, but because he believes he is not. If it is by faith that we receive salvation, then faith cannot be the assurance that we are already saved.

Conclusion:

All of these considerations constrain us to distinguish very clearly between saving faith and assurance of salvation. But if this distinction is valid, an important lesson clearly follows. *If saving faith is not assurance of salvation, then it is possible to challenge someone's assurance of salvation without undermining their faith.*

If assurance of salvation is not saving faith, then there may be such a thing as a counterfeit assurance of salvation and a counterfeit faith according to the Scriptures. If faith were the same as being assured of your salvation, then it would be wrong ever to tell someone to examine whether their assurance of salvation was genuine. *Because* that challenge would be equivalent to undermining their faith.

The Bible, however, in many places warns men about a false assurance of salvation:

> **Ephesians 5:5** For this you know with certainty, that no immoral or impure person or covetous man, who is an idolater, has an inheritance in the kingdom of Christ and God. 6 Let no one deceive you with empty words, for because of these things the wrath of God comes upon the sons of disobedience.

The reality of counterfeit faith is also clearly revealed in the Scriptures. There is such a thing as false faith (John 2:23-25; 8:30-33; Acts 8:13).

> **John 2:23:** Now when He was in Jerusalem at the Passover, during the feast, many believed in His name, observing His signs which He was doing. [24] But Jesus, on His part, was not entrusting Himself to them, for He knew all men, and because He did not need anyone to testify concerning man, for He Himself knew what was in man.

By revealing to us in His Word that there is such a thing as false or counterfeit faith, God confronts us unavoidably with the question, "Is my faith genuine or counterfeit?" If we are in earnest about our souls, this question cannot be avoided or evaded. In a later chapter I will discuss how we can know the difference between genuine and false faith.

Several practical applications follow from these scriptural facts.

(1) These perspectives deliver us from unhelpful and misguided counsels about struggles over assurance. Evangelical teachers today often tell souls troubled over assurance, "Stop doubting God! Just trust God!" If faith were assurance of salvation, such exhortations would be logical and appropriate. Sometimes, however, the person is not so much doubting God as doubting himself.

(2) These perspectives deliver us from the mentality that opposes all self-examination and the use of evidences in the matter of assurance of salvation. This mentality is common among those who believe that saving faith is assurance of salvation. If faith is assurance of salvation, then anything that undermines this assurance undermines faith and must be bad and legalistic. Looking for evidences of grace is bad. Self-examination is bad. Searching preaching is bad. But saving faith is not assurance of salvation. What is bad for some people's assurance of salvation may not be bad for them at all. In fact, challenges to the genuineness of their assurance of salvation may assist them in coming to genuine faith and genuine assurance of salvation.

Before we end this chapter, let's review. We have seen that there is a kind of assurance that is essential to saving faith. It is the assurance that the gospel is true and that Christ will save me if I go to Him. This assurance is not the same thing, however, as assurance of salvation. To put this another way, the assurance of faith is not the same as the assurance of salvation. They are two different things. In the next chapter we continue with three more important assertions about saving faith.

CHAPTER 17:

ON THE ASSURANCE OF FAITH—THE TARGET (CONTINUED)

In this chapter we continue with the subject of the assurance of faith and the assurance of salvation. Having looked at the outer two concentric rings in the target of assurance of salvation, that is, the first two assertions regarding assurance of faith and assurance of salvation, we come in this chapter to consider the inner three rings. The next and third assertion is this:

The seed of true assurance of salvation is present wherever there is true faith.

Faith is inseparable from at least some measure of assurance. Faith gives birth to—results in—some degree of assurance of salvation. This does mean that every believer has a prevailing assurance that overcomes all doubt and fear. It does mean that in the field of every believing heart the seed of assurance has been planted. How do we know this?

(1) This is so because the faith exercised at conversion receives the Spirit of adoption (Gal. 3:2 with 4:6). The Spirit of adoption, however, gives the seed of assurance. By it the adopted cry "Abba, Father" (Rom. 8:15; Gal. 4:6). Such a cry assumes that at some level the believer knows that God is His Father. This knowledge assumes some assurance of salvation.

(2) This may also be seen in the fact that every believer is marked by the grace of hope. Hope is one of the marks of election (1 Thess. 1:3, 4) and one of the results of the new birth (1 Pet. 1:3). Assurance is of the essence of hope and (the closely related concept) trust. Hope and trust are always personal in the Bible. It is hope for me in particular. Hope biblically is a personal, purifying, positive, confident expectation directed toward the unseen future, based on God and His Word (Heb. 6:19; 1 John 3:1-3).

> **Hebrews 6:19:** This hope we have as an anchor of the soul, a *hope* both sure and steadfast and one which enters within the veil,

> **1 John 3:1:** See how great a love the Father has bestowed on us, that we would be called children of God; and *such* we are. For this reason the world does not know us, because it did not know Him. 2 Beloved, now we are children of God, and it has not appeared as yet what we will be. We know that when He appears, we will be like Him, because we will see Him just as He is. 3 And everyone who has this hope *fixed* on Him purifies himself, just as He is pure.

Before going on to the fourth assertion, there is an important lesson for us here. The gospel of Christ is so free and gracious that it immediately imparts hope and the Spirit of adoption to every believer. One possible hindrance to true assurance of salvation is, then, a weak or obscure understanding of the freeness of grace and the immediacy of the justification provided in Christ. Is it possible that a failure really to understand and embrace the meaning of free grace and free justification through Christ alone is at the root of your struggles with assurance? This is a question that must be probed, if someone struggles with assurance of salvation.

There are degrees of assurance of salvation.

The fact that there are degrees of assertion is implied in the familiar hymn:

> Like a river glorious is God's perfect peace
> Over all victorious in its bright increase
> Perfect, yet it floweth fuller every day
> Perfect, yet it groweth deeper all the way

The assertion in the heading above follows from the previous one.

(1) If assurance of salvation is a matter of possessing the Spirit of adoption, then since we may have varying degrees of the filling of the Spirit, we may have varying degrees of assurance of salvation.

We as Christians may be filled with the Spirit (Eph. 5:18). We also may grieve the Spirit (Eph. 4:30). If we grieve the Spirit, it is possible to decrease our assurance of salvation. If we are filled with the Spirit, we may know more of it.

(2) Similarly, we have seen that assurance of salvation is of the essence of hope, but hope is a grace that may increase. Just as we may grow in faith and in love, so may we grow in the grace of hope. Remember Romans 15:13: "Now may the God of hope fill you with all joy and peace in believing, so that you will abound in hope by the power of the Holy Spirit." More hope means, however, more assurance of salvation. This is why the Bible exhorts us to make our calling and election sure (2 Pet. 1:10). The context of 2 Peter 1:10 is an exhortation to grow in grace (cf. vv. 5-9). By growing in grace (and, thus, growing in the grace of hope), we may grow in assurance of salvation.

Several practical lessons flow from this assertion:

(1) Assurance of salvation is not an all or nothing matter. Every Christian has some assurance. Every Christian may have more.

(2) You are not doomed to your present measure of assurance of salvation. As you may grow in grace, so you may grow in assurance of salvation.

(3) Assurance is not an arbitrary matter.

Of course, God is sovereign over everything including assurance of salvation. And just as many factors may affect our feelings, so many factors beside our spiritual health may impact our assurance of salvation. Yet, God bestows increased assurance in the use of the ordinary means, and its withdrawal is often associated with carelessness and sin. Speaking of assurance of salvation, the 1689 Baptist Confession in chapter 18, paragraph 3 says that the Christian "may, without extraordinary revelation, in the right use of means, attain thereunto: and therefore it is the duty of every one to give all diligence to make his calling and election sure ..."

We now come to the innermost circle on the target of assurance of salvation. It follows logically.

The marks of grace may be an important aid in attaining a prevailing assurance of salvation.

Because growth in grace can help one to grow in assurance of salvation, it follows that there are marks of grace that can help us to discern that we are Christians. This is both a biblical doctrine and one that can assist in attaining a prevailing assurance of salvation. One may, of course, attain a high and prevailing assurance of salvation immediately upon believing the gospel. Yet sometimes true Christians will wonder if their faith is genuine or false. This may be especially true for those Christians raised in a Christian home and who do not have a dramatic conversion experience. In such a case the doctrine of the evidences or marks of grace may be a wonderful assistance to attaining a prevailing assurance of salvation.

Let me illustrate what I mean by the marks of grace from a passage that was very helpful to me in this matter. That passage is 1 John 3:14: "We know that we have passed out of death into life, because we love the brethren. He who does not love abides in death."

I was raised in a Christian home and was first concerned for my salvation when I was very young. Yet I never was able to attain a prevailing assurance of salvation until I was in college. Some of the reasons were these. The doctrinal climate of the church in which I was raised was tainted by the idea that one could be saved and yet show no marks of grace. It was also distorted by the idea that our own free will and spiritual activity was the ultimate cause of our salvation.

Partly because of this, and partly because I was raised in a Christian home and did not have a dramatic conversion experience, I struggled to attain a prevailing assurance of salvation for many years. Later I learned, while I was in college, that salvation was all of grace—and not a matter ultimately of human decision or free will. I also learned that wherever God graciously touched a heart, there were marks or evidences that remained in the person's heart and life. You may think of these as the fingerprints of God left forever on that heart. I applied this new understanding to myself and shortly came to a wonderful assurance of salvation.

So God used what theologians have called the "practical syllogism" to impart to me assurance of salvation (A syllogism is a piece of logic). My particular use of the practical syllogism was based on 1 John 3:14. One way of stating a syllogism is this:

> If P, then Q. P therefore Q.
>
> If P—*If we love the brethren*
> Then Q—*Then we have passed out of death into life*
> P—*I do love the brethren*
> Therefore Q—*I have passed out of death into life*

This practical syllogism must, of course, never be taken out of the orbit of grace. If it is, it quickly can become a legalistic snare. It must always be connected with an understanding that it is grace alone, Christ alone, and faith alone that saves. Where, however, this is constantly kept in mind this syllogism may be of enormous assistance in coming to assurance of salvation. I hope it helps you.

Before this chapter is concluded, let me briefly review the five assertions I have made about the assurance of faith and assurance of salvation.

(1) There is a kind of assurance that is the essence of faith.

(2) Assurance of salvation is, however, not of the essence of saving faith.

(3)The seed of true assurance of salvation is present wherever there is true faith.

(4) There are degrees of assurance of salvation.

(5) The marks of grace may be an important aid in attaining a prevailing assurance of salvation.

CHAPTER 18:

ON THE AUTHENTICITY OF FAITH

In earlier chapters I have a couple of times commented on the subject of false and true faith. I said, for instance, that there was such a thing as false faith and false assurance of salvation. Previously I have said that I did not think that the difference between false and true faith was the difference between conviction of the truth of the gospel and commitment to the Christ of the gospel. The Bible, as we have seen, describes true faith in both ways.

Before I draw this little book to a close, I believe it is my responsibility to help you understand the difference between true or authentic faith and false or counterfeit faith. How else will you be able to be sure that you have done the two things you must do to be saved? How else can you help other people be sure they have?

The Bible itself gives very clear descriptions of counterfeit faith and how it differs from true faith. In this chapter I want to show you the fundamental distinction between authentic and counterfeit faith. Then I will explain the threefold differentiation of true faith as opposed to false faith.

The Fundamental Distinction

The fundamental distinction between authentic and counterfeit faith is that true faith is faith of and from the heart, while false faith is superficial and surface. Notice this emphasis in Paul's important description of saving faith in Romans 10:9-10.

> 9 that if you confess with your mouth Jesus *as* Lord, and believe in
> your heart that God raised Him from the dead, you will be saved;
> 10 for with the heart a person believes, resulting in righteousness,
> and with the mouth he confesses, resulting in salvation.

Twice Paul emphasizes here that the faith which saves is a heart faith. It is believing "in your heart" and "with the heart."

A similar emphasis emerges from Jesus' parable of the four soils. In His description of the second soil, we see the importance of the heart. This comes out in Jesus' emphasis that the seed must have deep soil and deep roots and not remain on the surface of a person's soul. Notice the following selections from that parable as found in Matthew 13.

> 5 "Others fell on the rocky places, where they did not have much soil; and immediately they sprang up, because they had no depth of soil. 6 "But when the sun had risen, they were scorched; and because they had no root, they withered away. .... 20 "The one on whom seed was sown on the rocky places, this is the man who hears the word and immediately receives it with joy; 21 yet he has no *firm* root in himself, but is *only* temporary, and when affliction or persecution arises because of the word, immediately he falls away.

On the other hand, the fourth soil represents those who are truly saved by the gospel. It emphasizes that the great fruit that this fourth soil bears comes from a "honest and good *heart*." Luke 8's account of the same parable emphasizes this.

> 15 "But the *seed* in the good soil, these are the ones who have heard the word in an honest and good heart, and hold it fast, and bear fruit with perseverance.

When I think of this matter of the importance of the heart, it reminds of Big Spring in the upper peninsula of Michigan. The small lake created by Big Spring was so clear you could see all the way to the bottom—even though it was 40 feet deep. When you took the small raft across the pool, you could actually see the water bubbling up out of the spring at the bottom of the pool.

The spring at the bottom of this pool is like the heart. It is the true spring of the thoughts, desires, and life of men. From it bubbles up all that makes a man truly who he is.

> **Proverbs 4:23:** Watch over your heart with all diligence, For from it *flow* the springs of life.

> **Matthew 12:34:** You brood of vipers, how can you, being evil,

> speak what is good? For the mouth speaks out of that which fills the heart.
>
> **Matthew 15:18-19:** But the things that proceed out of the mouth come from the heart, and those defile the man. For out of the heart come evil thoughts, murders, adulteries, fornications, thefts, false witness, slanders.

One might pour water colored with red dye into Big Spring, but it would quickly return to its original state as the red water flowed away and the spring at its bottom continued to fill it with crystal clear water. Just so one may pour the red dye of the gospel into a man's heart and create a surface and superficial faith, but unless the gospel takes possession of and changes the heart-spring of the person it will not fundamentally change the character of the pool of his life.

The faith of the heart is, then, a faith that is like the water which bubbles up out of that spring in the bottom of the pool. Surface or false faith is like water dumped into the top of the pool which quickly dissipates and does not affect the real nature of the pool.

It is important to remember that true faith is heart faith. There is something about such faith which authenticates itself. The kind of convictions and commitments that are less than whole-hearted and whole-souled do not bring true peace to the person, but when someone finally and unconditionally surrenders to Jesus there is a peace and release and confidence that often bubbles up in an immediate assurance that "Jesus is mine!"

Still, there are further indicators or manifestations of true faith as opposed to false. What are these tell-tale signs that reveal a heart faith as opposed to a mere, surface faith? That question is why we must go on to examine the next point.

The Threefold Differentiation

True faith is lasting, while false faith is often temporary.

One clear difference between true and false faith is that false faith often fades away, while true faith continues and perseveres.

The Bible describes true faith as lasting, while false faith if often temporary and impermanent. Matthew 13's description of the second soil emphasizes this:

> [21] yet he has no *firm* root in himself, but is *only* temporary, and when affliction or persecution arises because of the word, immediately he falls away.

John 6 also emphasizes that false faith is often marked by its final departure from Christ. In contrast those who have true faith feel they have no choice but to continue on with Jesus.

> [60] Therefore many of His disciples, when they heard *this* said,
> "This is a difficult statement; who can listen to it?" [61] But Jesus,
> conscious that His disciples grumbled at this, said to them, "Does
> this cause you to stumble? [62] *What* then if you see the Son of Man
> ascending to where He was before? [63] It is the Spirit who gives life;
> the flesh profits nothing; the words that I have spoken to you are
> spirit and are life. [64] But there are some of you who do not believe."
> For Jesus knew from the beginning who they were who did not
> believe, and who it was that would betray Him. [65] And He was
> saying, "For this reason I have said to you, that no one can come to
> Me unless it has been granted him from the Father." [66] As a result
> of this many of His disciples withdrew and were not walking with
> Him anymore. [67] So Jesus said to the twelve, "You do not want to
> go away also, do you?" [68] Simon Peter answered Him, "Lord, to
> whom shall we go? You have words of eternal life. [69] We have believed and have come to know that You are the Holy One of God."

Similarly, John 8 emphasizes the necessity of continuing to believe Christ's word as a mark of true faith and discipleship.

> [31] So Jesus was saying to those Jews who had believed Him, "If you
> continue in My word, *then* you are truly disciples of Mine; [32] and
> you will know the truth, and the truth will make you free."

Before leaving this first mark of true faith, a couple of practical comments need to be made.

First, while true faith always continues, false faith does not always fade completely away. The parable of the soils makes clear that some false believers maintain an outward profession, while withering into an unfruitful profession. Merely maintaining a kind of lip-service faith to Jesus is no sure sign of true faith. Remember the third soil in Matthew 13:

> 22 "And the one on whom seed was sown among the thorns, this is the man who hears the word, and the worry of the world and the deceitfulness of wealth choke the word, and it becomes unfruitful.

Second, and following from the first comment, perseverance is not the only sign of true faith. If it were the only sign of true faith, then assurance of salvation would be impossible in this life. You would have to persevere before you could be sure you have true faith. This would make assurance of salvation impossible.

Third, if a person's faith is only temporary and fades away, it is a clear indication that they never had true faith. The faith of the heart is always lasting and takes persevering possession of a person's soul. If a faith does not last, that is a sure sign that it is false.

True faith is fruitful, while false faith is dead.

The Bible describes true faith as living, active, and accompanied by other graces, while false faith as lifeless, inactive, and isolated from other graces. Galatians 5 sets before us Paul's description of the kind of faith which means something in Christ Jesus. The kind of faith which saves is a faith which is fruitful in good works.

> 6 For in Christ Jesus neither circumcision nor uncircumcision means anything, but faith working through love.

Similarly that classic passage which exposes the reality of a false faith emphasizes this. James 2 asks if an unfruitful faith can save someone. The answer is clearly no!:

> 14 What use is it, my brethren, if someone says he has faith but he
> has no works? Can that faith save him? .... 17 Even so faith, if it has

> no works, is dead, *being* by itself. .... [19] You believe that God is one. You do well; the demons also believe, and shudder. [20] But are you willing to recognize, you foolish fellow, that faith without works is useless? .... [26] For just as the body without *the* spirit is dead, so also faith without works is dead.

True faith is universal, while false faith is partial.

This heading needs a little explaining. I do not mean that true faith produces perfection in the true believer. What I mean is that true faith has a universal regard for everything Christ says. One indicator of false faith is that it has only a partial respect for Christ's words and does not regard all of Christ's commandments as true and binding. The supposed disciples of John 6 showed such a partial faith:

> [60] Therefore many of His disciples, when they heard *this* said, "This is a difficult statement; who can listen to it?" [61] But Jesus, conscious that His disciples grumbled at this, said to them, "Does this cause you to stumble? [62] "*What* then if you see the Son of Man ascending to where He was before? [63] "It is the Spirit who gives life; the flesh profits nothing; the words that I have spoken to you are spirit and are life. [64] "But there are some of you who do not believe." For Jesus knew from the beginning who they were who did not believe, and who it was that would betray Him. [65] And He was saying, "For this reason I have said to you, that no one can come to Me unless it has been granted him from the Father." [66] As a result of this many of His disciples withdrew and were not walking with Him anymore. [67] So Jesus said to the twelve, "You do not want to go away also, do you?" [68] Simon Peter answered Him, "Lord, to whom shall we go? You have words of eternal life. [69] We have believed and have come to know that You are the Holy One of God."

On the other hand, true disciples of Christ listen and follow him in everything He says. Acts 3 speaks of Jesus as the great prophet prophesied to come by Moses. It requires that all the words of this prophet be heeded. Otherwise that person who does not listen to everything he says must have no part in His people.

> 22 "Moses said, 'THE LORD GOD WILL RAISE UP FOR YOU A PROPHET LIKE ME FROM YOUR BRETHREN; TO HIM YOU SHALL GIVE HEED to everything He says to you. 23 'And it will be that every soul that does not heed that prophet shall be utterly destroyed from among the people.'

Psalm 119 beautifully illustrates this trait of faith (Cf. vv. 6, 13, 66, 80, 86, 101, 104, 128, 160, 172). Notice, for instance, the sentiments of the true believer in verse 128 of this Psalm: "Therefore I esteem right all *Your* precepts concerning everything, I hate every false way."

So again the "universal" nature of true faith does not mean that the one who has it lives a perfect life. Far from it! It does mean, however, that the true believer is convinced everything Jesus said is true and that everything He commanded is to be obeyed. The true believer does not pick and choose between Christ's words or between Christ's doctrines. This faith means that he sincerely endeavors to keep all of Christ's words and ultimately repents whenever he realizes he has failed to do so.

Conclusion:

This, then, is the difference between true and false faith. True faith is the faith of the heart. As the faith of the heart, it is lasting, fruitful, and universal. False faith is not, and there is a world of difference between authentic and counterfeit faith. The one with a heart conviction of the truth of the gospel and a heart commitment to the Christ of the gospel has the witness of the Spirit of adoption and is marked by the lasting, fruitful, and universal character of his faith.

The bottom-line is this. You can know if you have saving faith. You can also know if you do not, if you will but be honest with yourself. There is a world of difference between the two. No, rather, the difference between the two is the difference between heaven and hell!

CHAPTER 19:

HAVE YOU DONE THE TWO THINGS?

My goal in this book has been to take the confusion out of what God requires of you and the people you talk to in order that you should be saved. I believe there are great and wonderful mysteries in the gospel, but one of those mysteries is not how we may be saved! I do not believe that God wants you to be confused or mystified about how you can be saved. He wants people to understand that he requires two inseparable but distinct things: repentance toward and faith toward the Lord Jesus Christ. I have labored by means of the examples of the tree of repentance and the arrow of faith to make these two things as clear to your minds as I possibly can.

But my goal is not just to make these things clear to your minds, but to plant them in your hearts. I want them in your hearts so that you who know the Lord can explain them accurately and powerfully to others. But I also want you to take the time to reflect on yourself. So let me simply ask the million dollar question. Have you done the two things? Remember, when I ask you this, that I speak of things that must be done with the heart. You cannot go through the motions or just do these things externally. The two things you must do must be done with the heart.

But they must be done! So I ask you right now again, *Have you done the two things?* If you cannot answer that question with a clear yes, may I entreat you and plead with you right now where you are to do the two things?

Repent toward God! Feel sorrow for your sin, understand that God will be merciful to you, change your mind about God, sin, and Christ, and determine by the grace God will give you to serve Christ.

Exercise faith toward the Lord Jesus Christ! From the heart be convinced of the truth of the gospel and entrust yourself to the Lord Jesus Christ.

If you do these things, God absolutely promises that you will be saved. Acts 16:31 clearly says, "Believe on the Lord Jesus Christ, and you will be saved." The promises of the gospel are not tentative but certain. But they do require without exception that you do the two things you must do to be saved!

AUTHOR'S BIOGRAPHY

Dr. Samuel E. Waldron is a noted pastor, author and teacher. He holds a Th.M from Grand Rapids Baptist Seminary and a Ph.D from Southern Seminary in Louisville, Kentucky. Among his many other books are *The End Times Made Simple* and *To Be Continued: Are the Miraculous Gifts for Today?*